Creation of the Modern Middle East

Syria

Creation of the Modern Middle East

Syria

John Morrison

Introduction by
Akbar Ahmed
School of International Service
American University

CHELSEA HOUSE
P U B L I S H E R S
A Haights Cross Communications Company
Philadelphia

Frontispiece: Saladin's Tomb, c. 1927
Saladin (1137–93) was sultan of Egypt and Syria (1175–93) and the most respected adversary of the Crusaders.

CHELSEA HOUSE PUBLISHERS

VP, New Product Development Sally Cheney
Director of Production Kim Shinners
Creative Manager Takeshi Takahashi
Manufacturing Manager Diann Grasse

Staff for SYRIA

Editor Lee Marcott
Production Editor Jaimie Winkler
Picture Researcher Sarah Bloom
Series and Cover Designer Keith Trego
Layout 21st Century Publishing and Communications, Inc.

A Haights Cross Communications Company

http://www.chelseahouse.com

3 5 7 9 8 6 4 2

Library of Congress Cataloging-in-Publication Data

Morrison, John F., 1929–
  Syria / John Morrison.
    p. cm.—(Creation of the modern Middle East)
Summary: A history of Syria, focusing on the country's role in the current
political climate of the modern Middle East.
Includes bibliographical references and index.
  ISBN 0-7910-6509-X
  1. Syria—Juvenile literature. [1. Syria.] I. Title. II. Series.
DS93 .M58 2002
956.91—dc21
                                                      2002010572

Table of Contents

Index to the Photographs

Creation of the Modern Middle East

Iran

Iraq

Israel

Jordan

The Kurds

Kuwait

Oman

Palestinian Authority

Saudi Arabia

Syria

Turkey

Yemen

Introduction

Akbar Ahmed

The Middle East, it seems, is always in the news. Unfortunately, most of the news is of a troubling kind. Stories of suicide bombers, hijackers, street demonstrations, and ongoing violent conflict dominate these reports. The conflict draws in people living in lands far from the Middle East; some support one group, some support another, often on the basis of kinship or affinity and not on the merits of the case.

The Middle East is often identified with the Arabs. The region is seen as peopled by Arabs speaking Arabic and belonging to the Islamic faith. The stereotype of the Arab oil sheikh is a part of contemporary culture. But both of these images—that the Middle East is in perpetual anarchy and that it has an exclusive Arab identity— are oversimplifications of the region's complex contemporary reality.

In reality, the Middle East is an area that straddles Africa and Asia and has a combined population of over 200 million people inhabiting over twenty countries. It is a region that draws the entire world into its politics and, above all, it is the land that is the birth place of the three great Abrahamic faiths—Judaism, Christianity, and Islam. The city of Jerusalem is the point at which these three faiths come together and also where they tragically confront one another.

It is for these reasons that knowledge of the Middle East will remain of importance and that news from it will remain ongoing and interesting.

Let us consider the stereotype of the Middle East as a land of constant anarchy. It is easy to forget that some of the greatest lawgivers and people of peace were born, lived, and died here. In the Abrahamic tradition these names are a glorious roll call of human history—Abraham, Moses, Jesus, and Muhammad. In the tradition of the Middle East, where these names are especially revered, people often add the blessing "Peace be upon him" when speaking their names.

The land is clearly one that is shared by the great faiths. While it has a dominant Muslim character because of the large Muslim population, its Jewish and Christian presence must not be underestimated. Indeed, it is the dynamics of the relationships between the three faiths that allow us to enter the Middle East today and appreciate the points where these faiths come together or are in conflict.

To understand the predicament in which the people of the Middle East find themselves today, it is well to keep the facts of history before us. History is never far from the minds of the people in this region. Memories of the first great Arab dynasty, the Umayyads (661-750), based in Damascus, and the even greater one of the Abbasids (750-1258), based in Baghdad, are still kept alive in books and folklore. For the Arabs, their history, their culture, their tradition, their language, and above all their religion, provide them with a rich source of pride; but the glory of the past contrasts with the reality and powerlessness of contemporary life.

Many Arabs have blamed past rulers for their current situation beginning with the Ottomans who ruled them until World War I and then the European powers that divided their lands. When they achieved independence after World War II they discovered that the artificial boundaries created by the European powers cut across tribes and clans. Today, too, they complain that a form of Western imperialism still dominates their politics and rulers.

Again, while it is true that Arab history and Arab temperament have colored the Middle East strongly, there are other distinct peoples who have made a significant contribution to the culture of the region. Turkey is one such non-Arab nation with its own language, culture, and contribution to the region through the influence of the Ottoman Empire. Memories of that period for the Arabs are mixed, but what cannot be denied are the spectacular administrative and architectural achievements of the Ottomans. It is the longest dynasty in world history, beginning in 1300 and ending after World War I in 1922, when Kemal Ataturk wished to reject the past on the way to creating a modern Turkey.

Similarly, Iran is another non-Arab country with its own rich language and culture. Based in the minority sect of Islam, the Shia, Iran has often been in opposition to its Sunni neighbors, both Arab and Turk. Perhaps this confrontation helped to forge a unique Iranian, or Persian, cultural identity that, in turn, created the brilliant art, architecture, and poetry under the Safawids (1501-1722). The Safawid period also saw the establishment of the principle of interference or participation—depending on one's perspective—in matters of the state by the religious clerics. So while the Ayatollah Khomeini was very much a late 20th century figure, he was nonetheless reflecting the patterns of Iranian history.

Israel, too, represents an ancient, non-Arabic, cultural and religious tradition. Indeed, its very name is linked to the tribes that figure prominently in the stories of the Bible and it is through Jewish tradition that memory of the great biblical patriarchs like Abraham and Moses is kept alive. History is not a matter of years, but of millennia, in the Middle East.

Perhaps nothing has evoked as much emotional and political controversy among the Arabs as the creation of the state of Israel in 1948. With it came ideas of democracy and modern culture that seemed alien to many Arabs. Many saw the wars that followed stir further conflict and hatred; they also saw the wars as an inevitable clash between Islam and Judaism.

It is therefore important to make a comment on Islam and Judaism. The roots of prejudice against Jews can be anti-Semitic, anti-Judaic, and anti-Zionist. The prejudice may combine all three and there is often a degree of overlap. But in the case of the Arabs, the matter is more complicated because, by definition, Arabs cannot be anti-Semitic because they themselves are considered Semites. They cannot be anti-Judaic, because Islam recognizes the Jews as "people of the Book."

What this leaves us with is the clash between the political philosophy of Zionism, which is the establishment of a Jewish nation in Palestine, and Arab thought. The antagonism of the Arabs to Israel may result in the blurring of lines. A way must be found by Arabs and Israelis to live side by side in peace. Perhaps recognition of the common Abrahamic tradition is one way forward.

The hostility to Israel partly explains the negative coverage the Arabs get in the Western media. Arab Muslims are often accused of being anarchic and barbaric due to the violence of the Middle East. Yet, their history has produced some of the greatest figures in history.

Consider the example of Sultan Salahuddin Ayyoubi, popularly called Saladin in Western literature. Saladin had vowed to take revenge for the bloody massacres that the Crusaders had indulged in when they took Jerusalem in 1099. According to a European eyewitness account the blood in the streets was so deep that it came up to the knees of the horsemen.

Yet, when Saladin took Jerusalem in 1187, he showed the essential compassion and tolerance that is at the heart of the Abrahamic faiths. He not only released the prisoners after ransom, as was the custom, but paid for those who were too poor to afford any ransom. His nobles and commanders were furious that he had not taken a bloody revenge. Saladin is still remembered in the bazaars and villages as a leader of great learning and compassion. When contemporary leaders are compared to Saladin, they are usually found wanting. One reason may be that the problems of the region are daunting.

The Middle East faces three major problems that will need solutions in the twenty-first century. These problems affect society and politics and need to be tackled by the rulers in those lands and all other people interested in creating a degree of dialogue and participation.

The first of the problems is that of democracy. Although democracy is practiced in some form in a number of the Arab countries, for the majority of ordinary people there is little sense of participation in their government. The frustration of helplessness in the face of an indifferent bureaucracy at the lower levels of administration is easily converted to violence. The indifference of the state to the pressing needs of the "street" means that other non-governmental organizations can step in. Islamic organizations offering health and education programs to people in the shantytowns and villages have therefore emerged and flourished over the last decades.

The lack of democracy also means that the ruler becomes remote and autocratic over time as he consolidates his power. It is not uncommon for many rulers in the Middle East to pass on their rule to their son. Dynastic rule, whether kingly or based in a dictatorship, excludes ordinary people from a sense of participation in their own governance. They need to feel empowered. Muslims need to feel that they are able to participate in the process of government. They must feel that they are able to elect their leaders into office and if these leaders do not deliver on their promises, that they can throw them out. Too many of the rulers are nasty and brutish. Too many Muslim leaders are kings and military dictators. Many of them ensure that their sons or relatives stay on to perpetuate their dynastic rule.

With democracy, Muslim peoples will be able to better bridge the gaps that are widening between the rich and the poor. The sight of palatial mansions with security guards carrying automatic weapons standing outside them and, alongside, hovels teeming with starkly poor children is a common one in Muslim cities. The distribution of wealth must remain a priority of any democratic government.

The second problem in the Middle East that has wide ramifications in society is that of education. Although Islam emphasizes knowledge and learning, the sad reality is that the standards of education are unsatisfactory. In addition, the climate for scholarship and intellectual activity is discouraging. Scholars are too often silenced, jailed, or chased out of the country by the administration. The sycophants and the intelligence services whose only aim is to tell the ruler what he would like to hear, fill the vacuum.

Education needs to be vigorously reformed. The *madrassah,* or religious school, which is the institution that provides primary education for millions of boys in the Middle East, needs to be brought into line with the more prestigious Westernized schools reserved for the elite of the land. By allowing two distinct streams of education to develop, Muslim nations are encouraging the growth of two separate societies: a largely illiterate and frustrated population that is susceptible to leaders with simple answers to the world's problems and a small, Westernized, often corrupt and usually uncaring group of elite. The third problem facing the Middle East is that of representation in the mass media. Although this point is hard to pin down, the images in the media are creating problems of understanding and communication in the communities living in the Middle East. Muslims, for example, will always complain that they are depicted in negative stereotypes in the non-Arab media. The result of the media onslaught that plagues Muslims is the sense of anger on the one hand and the feeling of loss of dignity on the other. Few Muslims will discuss the media rationally. Greater Muslim participation in the media and greater interaction will help to solve the problem. But it is not so simple. The Israelis also complain of the stereotypes in the Arab media that depict them negatively.

Muslims are aware that their religious culture represents a civilization rich in compassion and tolerance. They are aware that given a period of stability in which they can grapple with the problems of democracy, education, and self-image they can take their rightful place in the community of nations. However painful the current reality, they do carry an idea of an ideal human society with them. Whether a Turk, or an Iranian, or an Arab, every Muslim is aware of the message that the prophet of Islam brought to this region in the seventh century. This message still has resonance for these societies. Here are words from the last address of the prophet spoken to his people:

> All of you descend from Adam and Adam was made of earth.
> There is no superiority for an Arab over a non-Arab nor for a
> non-Arab over an Arab, neither for a white man over a black man
> nor a black man over a white man . . . the noblest among you is the
> one who is most deeply conscious of God.

This is a noble and worthy message for the twenty-first century in the Middle East. Not only Muslims, but Jews, and Christians would agree with it. Perhaps its essential theme of tolerance, compassion, and equality can help to rediscover the wellsprings of tradition that can both inspire and unite.

It is for these reasons that I congratulate Chelsea House Publishers for taking the initiative in helping us to understand the Middle East through this series. The story of the Middle East is, in many profound ways, the story of human civilization.

— **Dr. Akbar S. Ahmed**
The Ibn Khaldun Chair of Islamic Studies and
Professor of International Relations,
School of International Service
American University

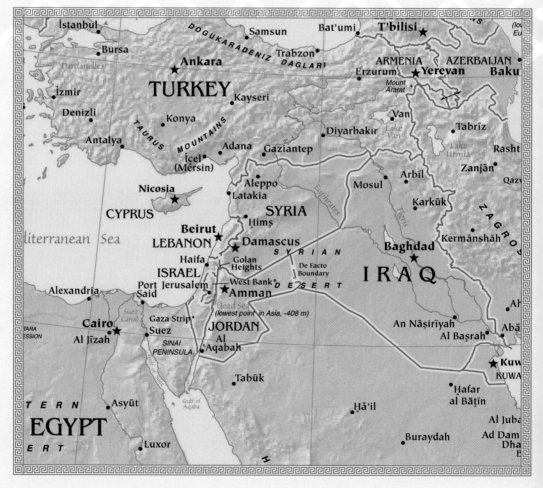

Map of Syria in the Middle East region

Modern map of Syria

Bashar Assad

Bashar Assad, trained as an ophthalmologist, succeeded his legendary father, Hafez Assad, as president of Syria in 2000.

1

After
the Lion

ashar Assad was too young to be president. The Syrian constitution said the president had to be 40 years old, and Bashar was only 34. But since his father, Hafez Assad, the man who had ruled Syria with an iron hand for 30 years, had chosen him as his successor, the constitution was quickly changed.

Hafez Assad died on June 10, 2000, while talking on the telephone to the president of Lebanon. Some observers saw symbolism in the way he died—a conversation unfinished, as he had left unfinished not only his part in peace negotiations with Israel, with whom Syria was still technically at war, but the process of bringing his troubled and underdeveloped country into the 21st century.

The question on everybody's mind that desperate June was

whether Bashar, the mild-mannered eye doctor and computer whiz with no military or government background to speak of, could carry on the legacy of the "Lion of Damascus" (*Assad* means "lion" in Arabic) while at the same time taking at least some steps in the direction of modernization of a country generally viewed as a "backwater" of the Middle East. In a *New York Times* article, Thomas L. Friedman described Syria at the time of Hafez's death as "the last country in the Middle East to introduce fax machines and the Internet, a country with a crumbling industrial base, a corrupt, 19th-century banking system, an utterly backward educational system, and not a single world-class export of any product or service"—a harsh indictment of the 30-year rule of Hafez Assad.

In addition, the country had long been on the United States' list of countries that support terrorism. Terrorist training camps had operated within Syria for many years, and its graduates went forth bent on the destruction of Israel and Israel's supporters. Although there was no evidence to link Syria with the September 11, 2001, attacks on New York City's World Trade Center and the Pentagon in Washington, D.C., the United States viewed any nation with links to terrorism as a possible threat. And it was not good policy to be on bad terms with the world's only remaining superpower.

Hafez Assad was 69 and afflicted with a variety of serious ailments when he died. Knowing death was near, he began to groom Bashar as his successor. It was well known that Assad would have preferred his eldest son, Basil, a dashing military officer, to rule after his death, but Basil had been killed in a car crash in 1994.

So, Bashar was brought home from England, where he had been practicing ophthalmology, to begin training as the new leader of a land that had been trampled over and mauled for 4,000 years by most of the mighty empires of the earth, where corruption and inefficiency were rampant, and where many powerful men were looking askance at this young man and wondering if he was up to the job.

During Bashar's "training," his father gave him diplomatic tasks to perform, and he was pushed onto the public stage as much as possible so that he would not be a total unknown when his father died. In addition, father and son purged the administration of those who objected to the planned succession.

Bashar followed in the footsteps of a man whose major accomplishment in three decades had been staying in power. Hafez Assad wasn't very good at much more than survival. As a military leader, he lost all the battles he fought with Israel. As a man of peace, he was too stubborn to make the concessions necessary to reach agreements among governments, even though he had committed himself to seeking peace. At the time of his death, a deal with Israel seemed tantalyzingly close.

But Hafez Assad knew how to keep a firm grip on power. He was ruthless in crushing his enemies and stifling dissent. He took control of a country that had endured 21 coups in as many years. Before Assad, government officials could barely get comfortable in their chairs before they were kicked out in favor of another equally incompetent group of leaders, who were shortly sent on their way as well. The coups may have been bloodless, but they kept this ancient country in a constant state of turmoil.

Hafez Assad ended this revolving-door style of government and brought stability and a sense of dignity to the Syrian people despite the harsh economic conditions under which many of them still lived.

When Assad's death was announced, the people crowded the streets of the capital city of Damascus and other Syrian cities and sent up an anguished chorus of

Hafez Assad, 1973

This photograph of Hafez Assad was taken in 1973, following the 1971 coup that led to his election as president the same year. He held that position for three decades, until his death in 2000.

regret. People cut themselves with knives, an expression of mourning. One woman rushed with the crowd to Assad's residence, beat her chest, and cried, "Say that he is not dead!"

An announcer on Damascus radio addressed the dead leader, saying, "Your soul is gone, but you are still with us."

Shops were shuttered, and the only business being done was by vendors selling long strips of black mourning cloth for banners and flags.

"It is like losing somebody very close," a 22-year-old laborer said of Hafez Assad. "I was one of his sons. The first thing I saw when I was born was President Assad." Would such warm sentiments be easily transferred to the new president? Only time would tell.

Meanwhile, Bashar's father's funeral brought heads of state or their representatives flocking to Damascus. In many Arab countries, flags flew at half-mast and official periods of mourning were declared. Even North Korea called a weeklong period of mourning.

The United States Secretary of State, Madeleine Albright, bowed her head briefly over Assad's casket. Palestinian leader Yasir Arafat, long a bitter enemy of Assad, saluted, then kissed Bashar and clung to his hand for several minutes of conversation.

Madeleine Albright emerged with a pledge from Bashar to follow in his father's footsteps: he agreed to continue the crucial peace talks with Israel. His father had agreed at a multilateral peace conference in Madrid in 1991 to consider peace negotiatons with Israel. But since he had stubbornly clung to his demand that the Golan Heights, lost to the Israelis in the Six-Day War of 1967, be returned to Syria, little progress had been made.

An article in the June 19, 2000 issue of *Newsweek* suggested that Assad had held out for one demand too many: "The main obstacle in Israeli-Syrian peace talks is but a few hundred disputed yards on the Sea of Galilee at the foot of the Golan Heights."

Former Israeli prime minister Shimon Peres commented, "Assad was always short a finger or two in reaching out to touch peace."

Because of such stubborness, there were no expressions

of mourning for Assad in Israel. A newspaper columnist wrote, "We Israelis have no reason to shed any tears over the death of Hafez Assad. It's a waste of water."

Such an attitude underlined the continuing hostility between the two countries that promised to make the struggle for a peace agreement a long, hard road, despite the arrival of a new man with, hopefully, new ideas on how to cope with the oldest and most intractable problem in the Middle East, and, by extension, the world.

After his funeral, Hafez Assad was laid to rest in his hometown, the tiny mountain village of Qardaha, 125 miles northwest of Damascus. Thousands of people milled around the mosque Assad had built to honor his mother. Soldiers struggled to keep mourners from pushing forward to kiss the flag-draped coffin so that prayers for the dead could begin. He was entombed next to his son Basil in a grand mausoleum on a hill over-looking the town.

Then, after the customary three days of mourning, Bashar Assad emerged to take the reins of a country whose problems would stagger, and had staggered, men of greater age and experience in the complex and confounding politics of the Middle East.

Photographs of Bashar Assad in military fatigues were plastered on walls, an indication of his desire for vital military support. Although he had little military experience, he held the rank of colonel. On ascending to the presidency, he was promoted to lieutenant general and became commander-in-chief of the military.

The mourners in the streets voiced their support for the new leader by chanting, "Bashar, we are with you!" Many of the young demonstrators had never known another regime except Hafez Assad's. They greeted the ascendancy of another Assad as the natural order of things.

On March 5, 2002, Syria announced its support of a

peace plan proposed by Crown Prince Abdullah of Saudi Arabia. The proposal promised peace for Israel and its neighbors if Israel would give back the territory it took from the Arabs in the 1967 war, including the Golan Heights. Bashar Assad met with Abdullah to discuss the plan, then announced the Syrian position. However, there didn't seem to be any likelihood that the Israelis would accept the plan, so the position was meaningless.

An earlier indication that Bashar was still strongly under the influence of the hard-liners in his government came when Syria used its first public appearance as a United Nations Security Council member, on January 19, 2002, to unleash a withering criticism of Israel.

Syria's U.N. representative, Fayssal Mekdad, assailed the destruction of Palestinian homes in Gaza by Israeli troops seeking to root out terrorists, and likened the action to the terrorist attacks on America, a connection not only absurd but extremely annoying to U.S. diplomats, who denounced it harshly.

Mekdad also defended anti-Israeli militants, criticized America's support of Israel, and urged the council to shift the focus of its counterterrorism campaign to Israel. It appeared to many that Syria continued to be preoccupied with Israel to the exclusion of other important considerations, and that it intended to try to stir up the rest of the world against the Israelis.

What does this tell the world about the policies of the new regime in Syria? Was it going to foster the same old discredited foreign policy? It seemed that young Bashar was afraid that if he did not appease the hard-liners, he might become a victim of another of those ceaseless coups that had plagued the country before his father took over.

He was certainly aware that despite the support of the people in the streets, and, for the moment at least, the backing of the military, there were those waiting in the

Syrian Protest, April 2002

Members of the Syrian National Socialist Party marched on the United Nations offices in Damascus in April 2002 to protest Israeli actions against Palestinians living in refugee camps in occupied territory. Israel was retaliating for Palestinian terrorists' suicide bombings against Israeli citizens.

wings, watching him carefully, and formulating their plans. Among them were not only his father's old enemies, but members of his own family, such as his angry uncle Rifaat, who had vowed to return from the exile into which his brother Hafez had sent him in order to take over the country. Even Bashar's younger brother Maher, who had made his career in the military, was waiting in the wings with his own ambitions.

How young Bashar would steer through the rocky path ahead of him was of vital interest not only to Syria and the Middle East, but to the world, since reverberations from conflicts in that dangerous region have always had, and will continue to have, an international impact.

Krack des Chevaliers (Arabic: Qual'at al-Hosn), c. 1910

The Krack des Chevaliers is the greatest of all Crusader castles. All that was best in both European and Middle Eastern military design combined to produce this masterpiece of military architecture.

2

Land of Abraham

Syria is a land of Bible stories. The very stones speak of history and legend. Muslims believe Damascus was the original Garden of Eden—that God fashioned Adam from the clay of the Barada River. It's where many believe the long centuries of man's fall from grace began when Adam and Eve were expelled from Paradise after tasting the forbidden fruit of the Tree of Knowledge. It is also where Cain is supposed to have killed Abel in the world's first murder, and hidden the corpse in a grotto. Abel's supposed tomb is outside Damascus, where a crimson streak of rock is said to be his blood spilling over the ground.

Syria's significance in religious history continues in the story of St. Paul, who, while on his way to Damascus from Jerusalem to fight the Christians, was knocked off his horse and blinded by a celestial light. A shrine was built six miles south of Damascus to mark the traditional place of his conversion. Here also Abraham was born and built an altar to his God. Moses and Lot and Job, figures from the Old Testament, prayed there. King David conquered here, as did Alexander the Great centuries later. The soldiers of many mighty empires marched over this ancient ground. All left their mark on the land and the people, who seemed forever to be altering their culture and religion to accommodate the new rulers.

Greater Syria once included what are now the countries of Israel, Jordan, and Lebanon, as well as parts of Turkey. But in 1918, following World War I, the region was carved up by the British, and Syria now is a nation of 71,498 square miles, bordered by Iraq, Jordan, Israel, and Turkey, with a short coastline on the Mediterranean Sea.

Its people are mostly Arabs, and the major religion is Islam, although there are other ethnic and religious minorities, including Christians. People who follow the religion of Islam (Arabic for "submission") are called Muslims (Arabic for "one who submits [to God]").

For centuries, camel caravans traveled back and forth across Syria, carrying goods between Asia and Mediterranean ports. As a result, Syrian cities like Damascus and Aleppo became major world trade centers as early as 2000 B.C.

The country is on the western end of the Fertile Crescent, so called because of its rich farmland. Thus, agriculture was a major industry in Syria for centuries, and still is an important part of the economy today. About half its population of some 16 million lives in rural areas. Some of these are Bedouins, nomads who live in tents and travel over the countryside with their livestock.

More than a million people live in Damascus, one of the world's most ancient cities. It is so old that no one really

Roman Citadel, Salahiyeh, c. 1916

Salahiyeh is a suburb southeast of Damascus. Excavations in this area during the 1950s demonstrated that an urban center flourished in this region during the fourth millennium B.C.

knows when it was first established. One legend holds that it was founded by Uz, great-grandson of Noah. Another says that it was begun by Demschak, a slave of Abraham. But those legendary tales only emphasize the mystery of the city's origins.

The Roman emperor Julian (361–363 A.D.) described it as " . . . the city which in very truth belongs to Zeus and is the eye of the whole east—sacred and most mighty Damascus."

But from the seventh century on, Damascus belonged to Allah. After centuries of being under the control of Akkadians, Canaanites, Arameans, Assyrians, Babylonians,

Persians, Greeks, Seleucids, Romans, and Byzantines, Syria was conquered in 636 A.D. by Muslim armies from the Arabian Peninsula.

One night early in 632 A.D., the prophet Muhammad, founder of Islam, called a servant to tell him he had received a summons from the dead in the graveyards of Medina, a city in what is now Saudi Arabia, to pray for them. The two went out into the night to find the cemetery, and, after his prayers, Muhammad predicted that he would soon die. At the time, Muhammad's Muslim armies were massed at the border of Syria, then under the control of the Christian Byzantine Empire, and were about to invade, but Muhammad became ill soon after his visit to the cemetery, and they decided to wait. Muhammad collapsed while leading Friday prayers, but he managed to raise himself up and tell his frightened people, "Has any prophet before me lived forever, that you thought I would never leave you? I return to him who sent me. My life has been good; so will be my death."

A few days later, he uttered his final words: "Oh, Allah, be it so! Henceforth among the glorious host of Paradise!" And the founder of what would become one of the world's major religions died. After his death, his armies, led by his disciple Abu Obeidah, invaded Syria and captured Damascus.

Within 20 years of Muhammad's death, his followers, obeying the principle of *jihad*, or holy war, had established the first Islamic empire in the Fertile Crescent, conquering the Persians and Byzantines, and within 100 years Muslims had created an empire that stretched from northern Spain to India. They were stopped from invading Western Europe in the Battle of Tours in 732 A.D.

The Muslims created a flourishing civilization in Iraq, Persia (now Iran), North Africa, Spain, and Syria. Culture and arts flourished. They built many magnificent structures, like the Alhambra in Spain and the Taj Mahal in India. Under Caliph Uthman, who ruled the Islamic world after Muhammad's death, the Koran—holy book of the Muslims (from an Arabic word meaning "recitation")—was put together from Muhammad's teachings.

Over the years, Muslims split into various sects. The two largest are the Sunni and the Shiite. Most Muslims, including those in Syria, are Sunnis. They believe that Muslim leadership after the death of Muhammad passed to caliphs elected from Muhammad's tribe, the Quraysh, which claimed descent from the Bible's Ishmael. The Shiites believe that leadership was restricted to descendants of Ali, Muhammad's son-in-law. These may seem like insignificant differences to outsiders, but to Muslims they are crucially important.

Muslims of all sects believe in one God, called Allah. The belief in one God was brought into Syria in the late 1200s B.C. by Hebrews. There is some irony in this, since the Arabs and the Jews, who share the belief in one deity, have been at odds for thousands of years.

The Koran includes stories from the Judeo-Christian Bible, and Muslims honor many of the same prophets, including the Old Testament patriarchs and Jesus. But they believe that Muhammad was the last of the prophets and that there will be no more.

The most ruthless of the many invaders of the Middle East had to have been the Christian Crusaders. In a series of invasions meant to wrest the Holy Lands from the "heathen" Muslims, the Crusaders felt compelled by religious fervor to slaughter Muslim men, women, and children, and did so with ruthless abandon.

In 1099, the Crusaders took Jerusalem after a 40-day siege and proceeded to kill most of the Muslim population. They didn't restrict their murderous onslaught to Muslims, however. They trapped a congregation of Jews in their synagogue, surrounded it, and burned it to the ground. They made sure every single Jew burned to death.

Roman Road Between Aleppo and Antioch, c. 1914

The ancient Romans constructed an outstanding road system throughout the Mediterranean world, extending from Britain to the Tigris and Euphrates Rivers and from the Danube River to Spain and northern Africa. In all, the Romans built more than 50,000 miles of hard-surfaced highways, primarily for military reasons.

   The Roman roads were notable for their straightness and solid foundations. They used concrete made from volcanic ash and lime. The Roman road system made possible the administration of their empire. Later, these roads provided the routes for the great migrations into the empire as well as a means for the diffusion of Christianity. Despite neglect, the Roman roads continued to serve Europe throughout the Middle Ages. Many fragments are still in use today.

     Similar depredations were carried out in Damascus. Abu Sa'ad al-Harawi, the *qyadii*, or senior judicial officer, in Damascus, was so shaken by sights of murder and destruction that he shaved his head in mourning. When he arrived at the palace of the Caliph al-Mustazhir in Baghdad to tell his tale, he was shocked to find the ruler and members of his court taking their ease in luxurious surroundings: "How dare you slumber in the shade of complacent safety, leading lives as frivolous as garden flowers, while your brothers in Syria have no dwelling place save the saddles of camels and the bellies of vultures?" he demanded. "Never have the Muslims been so humiliated. Never have their lands been so savagely devastated."

It wasn't until 1187 that the Kurdish warrior Salah-al-Din (Saladin), sultan of Egypt, who had created a powerful kingdom out of Egypt and Syria, defeated the Crusaders at the Battle of Hattin. Even though there was a third and final Crusade, the Christian intruders never again spread their conquest so far.

The history of Syria proceeded through the smoke of ceaseless blood and disaster for many centuries. In 1401 came the Mongol invader Timur (Tamerlane), who sacked and burned Damascus and Aleppo, setting back Syrian civilization and culture many decades.

Then arose the Turkish Ottoman Empire, which engulfed Syria in 1516, under the leadership of Sultan Selim I, and made Syria part of its vast empire. It held on until World War I, despite a brief intrusion by the Egyptians in the 1830s. (A combined force of British, Ottoman, and Austrian troops kicked the Egyptians out after only 10 years of control, and the Ottomans took over again.)

But the Ottomans made a big mistake at the outbreak of World War I by deciding to back Germany in the war, and it was this decision that led, after years of turmoil and discontent, to the eventual independence of the state of Syria.

Courtyard of the Zakariyah Mosque, Aleppo, c. 1920

The Zakariyah Mosque (built 715; rebuilt 1258) is named after Zacharias, the father of the biblical figure John the Baptist.

3

Lawrence of Arabia

*J*ust five feet, five-and-a-half inches tall, he was a little man. But he was as strong and tough as an Arabian saddle, and he had the endurance of a desert camel. In fact, it was said he could jump from a galloping camel while holding a heavy rifle and hop back on again in midstride.

He was Thomas Edward Lawrence, best known as T.E. Lawrence and "Lawrence of Arabia." He was the man who led the Arabs in many of the crucial battles that brought an end to the mighty Ottoman Empire during World War I and the liberation of the Middle East from the Turks and their German allies.

When he rode with his Arab forces into Damascus on October 1, 1918, to the wild acclaim of its citizens, it was the dramatic conclusion of a campaign that saw his desert forces, often battling against enormous odds, surge to a victory that would change the face of the Middle East forever.

The Ottoman Empire had ruled the Middle East since 1516, but it was doomed by its fateful decision to align itself with the wrong side—Germany—in World War I. As a result, it was consigned to the dustbin of history, with all the other once mighty empires that had ruled the Middle East over a span of 4,000 years.

What Lawrence, as a young English intelligence officer, brought to the Arabs in their fight against the Turks was British money and arms and the tactics of guerrilla warfare that enabled the Arabs to harass and confuse the Turkish and German forces.

A man of amazing courage, Lawrence—garbed in the flowing robes and headpiece of the Arabs, a curved dagger in his waistband, riding his favorite camel, Jedha—thundered into battle against artillery and machine-gun fire with reckless abandon. And he earned his Arabic nickname of *Emir Dinamit*, or Prince Dynamite, by blowing up railroad bridges to disrupt Turkish military transportation.

"For years we lived anyhow with one another in the naked desert, under the indifferent heaven," he wrote in his classic book, *Seven Pillars of Wisdom*. "By day the hot sun fermented us; and we were dizzied by the beating wind. At night we were stained by dew, and shamed into pettiness by the innumerable silences of stars.

"We were a self-centered army without parade or gesture, devoted to freedom, the second of man's creeds, a purpose so ravenous that it devoured all our strength, a hope so transcendent that our earlier ambitions faded in its glare."

He was a romantic and a poet. His *Seven Pillars of Wisdom* begins with a poem, part of which reads, "I drew these tides of men into my hands and wrote my will across the sky in stars. . . ."

But the horrors of battle were always with him and haunted his days and dreams for the rest of his eccentric life.

"Blood was always on our hands; we were licensed to it," he wrote. "Wounding and killing seemed ephemeral pains, so very brief and sore was life with us. With the sorrow of living so great, the sorrow of punishment had to be pitiless. We lived for the day and died for it. When there was reason and desire to punish we wrote our lesson with gun or whip immediately in the sullen flesh of the sufferer, and the case was beyond appeal. The desert did not afford the refined slow penalties of courts and jails."

One night early in the campaign, he and his wartime companion and friend, Feisal, a future king of Syria and later Iraq, were dining with the fierce Arab fighter Auda. Suddenly Auda leaped up with a cry of, "God forbid!"

He ran out of the tent, and soon the other diners heard a loud hammering. It was Auda pounding his false teeth to fragments on a stone.

"I had forgotten," he explained, "that Jemal Pasha (the Turkish commander in Syria who had hanged many Arab leaders) gave me these. I was eating my Lord Feisal's bread with Turkish teeth!" Fortunately, he had enough teeth left to finish the meal. But such was the ferocity of feeling against the hated Turks.

On Oct. 1, 1918, Lawrence rode into Damascus in his Rolls Royce with Feisal, Auda, and an array of other remarkable heroes, in advance of General Edmund Allenby's British Expeditionary Force. The night before, the victors had been shocked when they heard explosions in the city. They feared that the retreating German troops had set it on fire. But the next morning, Lawrence described the sight he saw:

"Instead of ruins, the silent gardens stood blurred green with river mist, in whose setting shimmered the city,

Waterwheel, Dayr az-Zawr, c. 1912

Dayr az-Zawr is a town in eastern Syria situated on the right bank of the Euphrates River. Under the Ottomans, it was the capital of an administrative region and the site of outposts for policing the surrounding country.

   A waterwheel is a mechanical device for tapping the energy of running or falling water by means of a set of paddles (left center). The force of the moving water against the paddles rotates the wheel and is transmitted to machinery via the shaft in the wheel (center). The waterwheel was the earliest source of mechanical energy to replace that of humans and animals.

beautiful as ever, like a pearl in the morning sun."

   Feisal was briefly the leader of a pan-Arab state based in Damascus. Hopes arose for the treasured ideal of Arab independence, which Lawrence, Feisal, and many other heroic men had fought for. They believed they had British assurances of independence once the Ottomans were defeated.

   Britain had promised to support an independent Arab state or a Confederation of Arab States before the war as a way of getting the Arabs to join the Allies in subduing the Germans and Turks. But the secret Sykes-Picot Agreement of May 16, 1916, later part of the postwar League of Nations mandates, granted Britain control of Iraq, Transjordan (later Jordan), and Palestine (which was separated from Greater Syria), and the French oversight of Syria and Lebanon. The existence of the Sykes-Picot Agreement was kept secret by the Western powers but was revealed later, by the Russians, following the 1917 Bolshevik Revolution.

Feisal had become king of Syria, but he was violently ousted by the French. As compensation, the British installed him as king of Iraq, then called Mesopotamia. His brother Abdullah became king of Transjordan.

Lawrence was seriously disillusioned by Feisal's ouster by the French. The brief moment of Syrian independence had kindled his hopes that his Arab brethren might indeed attain freedom. But despite this setback, he still had hope, because of one man—Winston Churchill.

Churchill, who was named British colonial secretary in 1921, asked Lawrence to advise him on Middle Eastern policy. But it was difficult for many of the professional British soldiers to take this brash young man seriously. In one encounter at the Majestic Hotel in Paris, headquarters of the British delegation at a peace conference in 1919, a British general confronted him. Lawrence tried treating the officer with mild respect, but the officer must have detected a note he didn't like in Lawrence's demeanor.

"Don't dare to speak to me in that tone," the general huffed. "You're not a professional soldier."

"No," Lawrence said, "perhaps I'm not, but if you had a division and I had a division, I know which of us would be taken prisoner."

Lawrence's acerbic sense of humor might have eased the strains of battle and diplomacy, but it tended to alienate some of the pompous officers he had to deal with.

Once, on a raid, Lawrence was compelled to leave his medical officer behind. The British surgeon general demanded in a telegram to know how Lawrence planned to deal with his wounded without a medical officer.

His telegraphed reply: "Will shoot all cases too hurt to ride off."

Lawrence had been so discouraged in 1919 by what he viewed as treachery by Britain and France in failing to give the Arabs independence that he refused to accept medals the British government wanted to give him. However, in his role of adviser to Churchill, Lawrence felt strides were made that would bring both peace and eventual independence to the troubled region.

"I take to myself credit for some of Mr. Churchill's pacification of the Middle East, for while he was carrying it out he had the help of such knowledge and energy as I possess," he wrote in a letter to an author of a book about the revolt in the desert. "His was the imagination and courage to take a fresh departure and enough skill and knowledge of political procedure to put his political revolution into operation in the Middle East. . . . When it was in working order, in March 1922, I felt that I had gained every point I wanted."

The Arabs, he felt, "had their chance and it was up to them, if they were good enough, to make their own mistakes and profit by them."

But not everybody shared Lawrence's optimism for lasting peace for the region. Field Marshall Earl Wavell parodied the famous saying that World War I was a "war to end all wars" by commenting that the state of affairs after the war was a "peace to end all peace." Britain and France had carved up the Middle East without regard to the needs and desires of the Arab population. For example, the Kurds were originally promised their own homeland, but they ended up as part of both Iraq and Turkey, where they still continue their struggle for independence. Originally, the two Ottoman provinces of Basra and Baghdad comprised Iraq. Later Britain added the oil-bearing province of Mosul

Threshing, Mismiyeh (Ancient Phaena), Hauran Area, c. 1920
This threshing machine is separating the grain (left) from straw (right).

in the north, dashing the Kurds' hopes and angering the Sunni and Shiite Muslim sects.

Journalists Pierre Salinger and Erik Laurent commented, "Iraq was created by Churchill, who had the mad idea of joining two widely separated oil wells, Kirkuk and Mosul, by uniting three widely separated peoples: the Kurds, the Sunnis and the Shiites." And Churchill liked to brag that he had created Transjordan with the stroke of a pen and then had time in the afternoon to paint a landscape

Meanwhile, another situation was turning into early violence. In 1917, British foreign secretary Arthur Balfour sent a letter to Lord Rothschild, a leading British Zionist, pledging Britain's support for a national homeland for the Jewish people in Palestine. (Zionism was a movement begun in the 19th century that sought to achieve a Jewish homeland in Palestine.) Known as the Balfour Declaration, it led inevitably to clashes between the Jews and Arabs that continue into the 21st century.

While the Jewish "problem" was not paramount in T.E. Lawrence's association with Churchill and the peace process after World War I, it had profound impact on the Middle East that emerged from the war.

One morning in 1921, when Churchill was touring the Middle East, he made a brief stop in Gaza, in Palestine, and was greeted by a cheering crowd. "Cheers for the Minister! Cheers for Great Britain!" the crowd chanted. What Churchill, who didn't understand Arabic, didn't hear were the even louder outcries: "Down with the Jews!" and "Cut their throats!"

Arab riots broke out throughout Palestine and in Jerusalem. In Haifa, police fired on a crowd, killing a 13-year-old Christian Arab boy and a Muslim Arab woman.

At a dinner with Emir Abdullah, future king of Jordan, Churchill said that while Jews would continue to be allowed to enter Palestine, "the rights of the existing non-Jewish population would be strictly preserved."

While Abdullah was optimistic, the rest of the Arab population was not. The Arabs petitioned Churchill to end Jewish immigration, at least until a Palestinian government could be established, but Churchill refused; he was bound by the Balfour Declaration. "It is manifestly right that the Jews, who are scattered all over the world, should have a national center and a national home where some of them may be reunited," he said. "And where else could that be but in this land of Palestine, with which for more than three thousand years they have been intimately and profoundly associated?"

To the Jews of Palestine, Churchill proclaimed that Zionism was a "great event in the world's destiny." The Jews, he said, would bring prosperity, "which would benefit all the inhabitants; no Arabs would be dispossessed."

Some of those statements seem extremely naïve considering events that gradually unfolded over the next 80 years.

Meanwhile, T.E. Lawrence continued to hope for a unified Arab territory whose center would be located in Baghdad rather than Damascus, because Syria had become a less significant region than Iraq. He was right about that, but there was to be no Arab union. It remained an elusive dream that not many in the Middle East even bother to entertain anymore.

After his work with Churchill, Lawrence withdrew from public life, although publication of his *Seven Pillars of Wisdom* and its acclaim as a masterpiece brought him back into the public eye briefly.

In 1922, he enlisted in the British Royal Air Force as a private and adopted new names, first J.H. Ross and later T.E. Shaw. No one knew why he changed his name, except that he didn't like acclaim and hid from the fame that other men would have treasured.

He never married and lived alone most of the time in an isolated cottage in Dorset. He died on May 19, 1935, after a motorcycle accident. He was 46.

Bedouins Eating in Front of Their Tent, Hauran Area, Southern Syria, 1923

Bedouins are an Arabic-speaking nomadic people of the Middle Eastern deserts. Most Bedouins are animal herders who migrate into the desert during the rainy season and move back to cultivated land in the dry summer months. In the 1950s, Syria nationalized Bedouin rangelands. Conflicts between Bedouin herders and settled agriculturists have increased since then.

4

A Taste
of Freedom

1 n one of his videotaped harangues against the West after the September 11, 2001, terrorist attacks on the New York World Trade Center and the Pentagon in Washington, D.C. terrorist boss Osama bin Laden had a message for the world. He said that what the American people had suffered in the attacks was nothing compared to what the Arabs had been suffering for more than 80 years.

His reference to 80 years took some people by surprise, since the usual Islamic complaint against the West refers to events going back at least 1,000 years. It sent some historians scrambling to find out what had happened "more than 80 years ago."

Of course, bin Laden meant the October 1917 Balfour Declaration

—an event seen by many Arabs as the source of eight decades of turmoil and despair.

Actually, it's not hard to see why the Arabs were harboring resentment over what they saw as a double double-cross by the West: first, the secret Sykes-Picot Agreement, in which Britain and France agreed to divide up the Middle East, and second, the Balfour Declaration and its promise of a Jewish homeland in Palestine.

At the time, there were 690,000 Arabs in Palestine, compared to 85,000 Jews. Within a couple of decades, Jews came to outnumber the Arabs, and they subsequently established their right to exist in three wars with their neighbors. Some 700,000 Palestinians went into exile, to the growing chagrin of their Middle Eastern neighbors, who had to take them in.

Actually, bin Laden should not have been as resentful as most. His homeland, Saudi Arabia, was left pretty much alone by the Allies after the war. Any problems the Saudis had were of their own making, not imposed by outside forces, as in Syria and the other Arab states. As T.E. Lawrence put it, they were free to make their own mistakes and learn from them.

But in the rest of the Arab world, external interference was the rule. In response to the Sykes-Picot agreement and the League of Nations mandate, French troops marched from Beirut to Damascus to take over Syria. The Arabs put up a fight, but they were overwhelmed. It wouldn't be the last time that French guns were turned on the Syrians before the final pullout of the French in 1946.

(During the years of World War II, French attention would turn to Germany and to domestic problems.)

The brief period of Syrian self-government after World War I, when Feisal was king, had given nationalists in the country a taste of freedom, and many continued to fight for that freedom against the French. Among those touching off the revolts was Ibrahim Hannanu, who incited a rebellion in July 1919. Although it and other resistance movements were brutally suppressed by the French, both Feisal and Hannanu have gone down in Syrian history as heroes of independence.

One important condition of the French mandate in Syria and Lebanon was that it was to be temporary, to allow for eventual independence. But the French appear to have lost sight of this specification. They ruled Syria with an iron hand; nearly every feature of Syrian life came under French control. Children were required to speak French and sing "La Marseillaise," France's national anthem. The franc became the currency of the economy, and currency management was in the hands of French bankers, who were more concerned with French share-holders and interests than with Syrian.

Meanwhile, the Arab nationalist movement in Syria was led by educated, wealthy Muslims whose grievances against the French included suppression of newspapers, political activity, and civil rights. The French set out to weaken this movement by dividing the country into separate regions and giving support to religious minorities. The nationalists were isolated in Damascus. There, they founded the People's Party, which demanded French recognition of eventual Syrian independence, as well as the granting of civil liberties.

Violence broke out in separate uprisings by Alawis, Druzes, and Bedouins, but these, like the other efforts at liberation, were put down by the French. A more serious rebellion by the Druzes occurred in 1925. The Druzes were an Islamic minority that controlled the Jabal Druze, a region in southern Syria. Their revolt against the French quickly spread throughout the country, igniting rebellions in Aleppo and Damascus. After heavy fighting, the French ended the revolt by the systematic bombardment of Damascus, killing about 5,000 Syrians.

Druze Boys, Southern Syria, 1893

The Druze is a small Middle Eastern religious sect. It is a secret religion that permits no conversion, either away from or to the sect. Only an elite group of believers participates fully in this strict monotheistic religion, which can be traced back at least a thousand years. In 2000, the Druze sect numbered about 250,000.

In 1928, the French allowed the formation of the National Bloc, composed of various nationalist groups centered in Damascus. It included leading members of large landowning families. The National Bloc wrote a constitution, which the French put into effect—after deleting all references to independence.

But the Syrian nationalists wanted a treaty with France that would spell out French intentions toward the country. Britain and Iraq had signed such a treaty in 1922. A general strike in 1936 helped persuade the French, under Leon Blum's liberal-socialist government, to negotiate such a treaty, called the Syrian-French Treaty of Alliance, that year. The French parliament never ratified the treaty, but the Syrians believed an important step had been taken for eventual self-rule.

The French weren't all bad. They made many physical improvements to the country, building roads and schools and helping to make Damascus and Aleppo into modern cities. They even trained some Syrians as minor bureaucrats.

Finally, with French approval, the first Syrian nationalist government came to power in 1936, with Hashim al Atassi, one of the founders of the National Bloc, as president.

But all this fell apart in 1939 when France agreed to hand over to Turkey the northern province of Alexandretta, later Hatay, a port on the Mediterranean with a large Turkish minority. Many Syrians blamed the Atassi government for the loss, and Atassi resigned. Parliamentary institutions were abolished, and France again governed the unruly country through a Council of Directors. It looked like Syria's second serious attempt at self-government had failed.

But Hitler's Germany was about to change everything. The Germans quickly conquered France in 1940 at the outset of World War II and set up the Vichy government to run France and carry out Hitler's policies.

This meant that Syria was now governed by Vichy France. But Vichy's hold on Syria was a fragile one. British and Free French forces under General Charles de Gaulle, combined with the Transjordan Arab Legion, defeated the Vichy forces in both Syria and Lebanon. De Gaulle promised eventual independence for Syria, but the French Mandate remained in effect even under the Free French.

De Gaulle felt that the mandate would have to be formally rescinded by a new French government after the defeat of the Nazis.

With the National Bloc now in control, Syrians elected a new parliament in 1943 and began taking over functions of the government, including those dealing with customs, social affairs, excise taxes, and other matters. The French retained control of social, cultural, and educational services, as well as of the peace-keeping force, called the Troupes Speciales du Levant. (The Levant consisted of Syria, Lebanon, and Palestine.)

But in July 1944, to the dismay of the French, the Soviet Union recognized Syria and Lebanon unconditionally as sovereign states. The United States followed in September, and British recognition followed a year later. These nations began pressuring France to get out of the region.

In January 1945, Syria belatedly entered World War II on the side of the Allies. It declared war on the Axis powers in February 1945, having formed a national army. In March, the country became a charter member of the United Nations.

But at the same time, Syria affirmed its allegiance to the idea of Arab unity by signing the pact of the League of Arab States.

The European phase of World War II ended in April 1945, but the French were not finished with Syria, and even more blood would be spilled before they vacated the region for good.

In May 1945, there were violent demonstrations against the French occupation in Damascus and Aleppo. Once again the French bombed and fired on the ancient capital. Serious fighting broke out in Homs and Hamah as well. It was only after Winston Churchill, then the British prime minister, threatened to send in troops to restore order that General de Gaulle ordered a cease-fire.

French control of Syria finally was grinding to a halt. In

Albanian Railroad Laborers, Deraa, 1907

The Hejaz Railroad between Damascus and Medina was one of the principal railroads of the Ottoman Empire.

Its main line (820 miles) was constructed between 1900 and 1908 both to facilitate pilgrimages to Muslim holy places and to strengthen Ottoman control over the far-flung empire. The railroad was built by a multiethnic labor force under the supervision of a German engineer. It ran from Damascus southward to Deraa and then across Transjordan to Arabia and Medina. A major branch line, about 100 miles long from Deraa to Haifa on the Mediterranean coast of Palestine, was completed in 1905.

February 1946, the United Nations passed a resolution calling on France to evacuate the country. The French agreed, and by April 15, 1946, all French troops were off Syrian soil.

On April 17, Syrians celebrated Evacuation Day. It became a national holiday.

But the celebration would be short-lived, as the effects of the Balfour Declaration soon would become apparent, dominating the attention of Syria as well as her Arab neighbors.

Under pressure from the Arabs, the British, signers of the Balfour Declaration, had begun severely limiting immigration of Jews into Palestine. In May 1939, Britain had issued a "white paper" that came close to repudiating the Balfour Declaration. It placed severe limitations on Jewish immigration and land purchases and accepted the Arab claim to self-determination.

But the British badly underestimated the determination of Jews worldwide, especially those from Europe. Europe was not only where the Nazis slaughtered six million Jews in the Holocaust, it was where Jews had been subjected to repeated pogroms and other outrages for centuries.

When an American riverboat, converted into a transport ship, sailed from Marseilles, France, in July 1947 loaded with Jewish refugees bound for Palestine and was prohibited from docking there by the British, the issue became one of worldwide concern. The ship, renamed *Exodus* by its passengers, became a symbol of the Jewish refugees' plight and Britain's consistent refusal to allow refugees to disembark in Palestine. But refugees did continue to pour into Palestine, to the continued frustration of the British and the murderous rage of the Arabs.

On November 29, 1947, the United Nations passed an historic resolution, partitioning Palestine into two independent states, one Jewish and one Arab. At midnight on

May 14, 1948, the Jews proclaimed the State of Israel. The combined actions would change the face of the Middle East forever and bring violence and bloodshed to a vast region of the globe.

Main Square, Damascus, c. 1930

The main railroad station occupied the buildings on the right. Hardly any trains now use the station, which was built by the Ottomans to transport pilgrims from Damascus to Medina.

5

Birth of
a Nation

ive Arab nations—Syria, Lebanon, Iraq, Egypt, and Jordan—were invading the new country even as Moshe Sharett, foreign minister of the State of Israel, was dispatching cables to other governments asking for recognition. And while the United States, with Harry S. Truman in the White House, was the first to recognize the new nation on May 15, 1948, and the Soviet Union followed three days later, the question on everyone's mind was whether one million Jews had any chance against a total Arab population of 40 million. Reliable estimates had put the combined strength of Egypt, Syria, Jordan, Iraq, Lebanon, and Saudi Arabia at 482,000 troops, 2,180 tanks, and 848 combat aircraft, while Israel's strength was estimated at 264,000 troops,

800 tanks, and 300 combat aircraft. The Saudis had sent a formation that fought under Egyptian command.

British prime minister Clement Attlee predicted Israel's doom. His biographer quoted him as saying, "If war broke out between Jews and Arabs, the Foreign Office and the British Chiefs of Staff reported categorically, the Arabs would throw the Jews into the sea."

Even David Ben-Gurion, Israeli prime minister, was gloomy. In proclaiming the State of Israel at a special session of the Jewish National Council of Palestine in Tel Aviv, Ben-Gurion admitted he was not in a celebratory mood. "I feel no gaiety in me," he said. "only deep anxiety, as on the 29th of November, when I was like a mourner at the feast." He referred to the day of the United Nations' resolution that partitioned Palestine into Jewish and Palestinian territories.

Arab chiefs of staff had held a meeting in Damascus in April 1948 to work out a coordinated offensive against Israel. According to the plan, Syrian and Lebanese armies were to invade northern Palestine and occupy Tiberias, Safed, and Nazareth. The main effort would be launched by the Iraqi army and the Arab Legion of Jordan south of Lake Tiberias. They would then move west toward the port of Haifa, which was seen as the main objective of the opening phase of the campaign. The Egyptians, including the Saudi Arabia contingent, were to pin down the Jewish forces south of Tel Aviv.

The plan looked good on paper, but in the field, chaos reigned.

King Abdullah of Jordan was supposed to be the overall commander of the Arab forces, but only his Arab Legion, the most efficient of all the armies, paid any attention to his orders. The Arab Legion was an elite force trained and equipped by the British with a British officer, Sir John Glubb ("Glubb Pasha") in command.

The other Arab armies went their own ways.

Abdullah had no interest in Haifa, which he felt was outside the territory of the Palestinian partition anyway. He had been warned by British foreign minister Ernest Bevin, "Don't go and invade the area allotted to the Jews." Abdullah took the warning seriously because he wanted to maintain good relations with the British, who still exerted a major influence on his country even though their mandate had expired.

Abdullah kept his forces in the West Bank territory designated by the United Nations for the Arab State, and surrounded Jerusalem, which had been declared an international city.

There was no coordinated attack. The Arab offensive was piecemeal, which greatly diminished Arab superiority in numbers and armament.

The Syrians attacked in the Jordan Valley in brigade strength, with an armored-car battalion, an artillery regiment, and a company of tanks. The valley was an area of heavy Jewish settlement. The Syrians captured the town of Zemah, and on May 20, attacked the Israeli settlements of Degania.

Degania was defended initially by only 70 men, armed with mortars and machine guns, and using Molotov cocktails against the Syrian tanks. The Syrian force also had some air support, but the bombers were so inaccurate they didn't have much effect on the battle.

Israel's Moshe Dayan set about bolstering the defensive line facing the Syrians. The Syrians attacked shortly after 4 A.M., but their tanks were knocked out by the Israelis' anti-tank bazookas and Molotov cocktails. Later, 65-mm guns arrived and began shelling the Syrian positions in Zemah. The supporting Syrian infantry, concealed in a barley field, heard the shriek of Israeli shells over their heads and fled in panic.

The Syrians evacuated Zemah. On an inspection tour the night of the battle, Dayan found that the fleeing Syrians had left behind weapons and vehicles scattered in the streets.

Arab Village, c. 1913

The British tourist who took this unusual photograph wrote the caption: "Arab Village, Syria."

  Note the village wall. The wall and the houses are made from limestone, and the houses are constructed without windows—keeping the temperature down during the hot summers.

"The battle was over," Dayan wrote, "a tough, tragic and depressing battle. Much young blood had been shed, the blood not of trained and experienced veteran warriors but of youngsters meeting death wide-eyed."

A truce agreement brokered by the United Nations ended the fighting temporarily in June 1948, but when it expired on July 9 there was renewed fighting between Israel and Egypt in the Negev Desert for ten days.

A final battle took place when the Israelis invaded the Sinai, held by Egypt. Ben-Gurion's reasoning in attacking the Sinai was to push the Egyptians further away from the Israeli

Arab Women, Syria, c. 1913

The same British tourist who took the preceding village photo also photographed these village women.

capital of Tel Aviv. This brought a strong reaction from Britain, which had a treaty with Egypt dating back to 1936.

During the fighting, British Royal Air Force planes flew over Israeli-held territory on reconnaissance and five of them were shot down by the Israelis. For a time, it almost looked as if Britain and Israel would be at war.

But the Egyptians turned away Britain's help and negotiated a treaty with Israel. This encouraged the other Arab countries to also seek armistice agreements. Most of them were negotiated without much problem through the U.N. secretary general Ralph Bunche.

But the talks with Syria bogged down because Syria wanted to retain some Israeli territory it still occupied along its border. Negotiations dragged into the summer of 1949. They were held in a stiflingly hot tent pitched on the Tiberias–Damascus highway, near Mishmar Hayarden, a no-man's land between the two camps.

After long argument, the Syrians agreed to withdraw their forces from Israeli territory on condition that a demilitarized zone be established there. The Israelis agreed, and an armistice was signed in July 1949.

Trouble started again when the Israelis insisted on continuing with some water resource development projects they had started, resulting in extensive digging and engineering that spilled over into the demilitarized zone.

Syria objected and complained to the U.N. that Israel had no right to work in that zone. When the Syrians received no satisfaction from the U.N., they began taking potshots across the border at workers in the zone. The U.N. Security Council passed a resolution calling for work to be suspended pending negotiations, which dragged on without resolution for years.

Overall, the armistice agreements between Israel and its Arab neighbors were hailed as a triumph for the United Nations, and many observers saw peaceful years ahead. But the sacred city of Jerusalem was left divided and would remain a subject of dispute for years ahead.

And the Arabs in general still hated the Jews and wanted them out of Palestine.

The peace treaties with Israel were a severe blow to Arab pride. For one thing, most Arab governments controlled the press in their countries, and the general population had been led to believe that the mighty Arab armies would run the Jews out of the region with little difficulty. The Arabs were shocked when they finally learned the truth—that Israel had staved off five powerful Arab countries and remained in solid control of the cherished region.

The year 1948 was called *al-nakba,* Arabic for "catastrophe," in the Arab nations, and those deemed responsible for it were made to suffer. In Egypt, Premier Nokrashy Pasha was assassinated at the end of December. King Farouk was ousted by a military coup.

King Abdullah of Jordan actually fared better than the other Arab leaders. In 1950, he merged Transjordan and the Arab-held part of Palestine, including the Old City of Jerusalem, into the Hashemite Kingdom of Jordan. The Hashemites were a family that traced its lineage back to the Prophet Muhammad.

But Abdullah was assassinated on July 20, 1951, after Friday prayers at the mosque of al-Aqsa in the Old City.

In Syria, the first of many military coups was launched by Colonel Husni Zaim, the head of the Syrian army, who ousted the government of Shukri al-Quwwatli. The military blamed him for losing the war.

Thus began years of turmoil for Syria, which actually had been in ferment almost since the French pulled out in 1946.

Ba'ath Party Conference, 2000

Syria's ruling Ba'ath Party, shown here in session in June 2000, was founded in 1940 to represent the interests of Syria's growing middle class; it endured many challenges to its policies and authority in the ensuing years until it ascended to power along with Hafez Assad.

6

The Arabs Unite

S yria had actually been a mess since Evacuation Day in 1946. The country had been fairly stable with outside enemies to struggle against. In modern times, there had been the Ottoman Empire, then the French, then the Israelis. Faced with a common enemy, the many religious and political factions in the country had gotten along. But when their primary enterprise became governing themselves, things fell apart.

After the French pulled out in 1946, Syria tried a parliamentary democracy. In such a system, a prime minister runs the country and is answerable to a parliament, which makes the laws. It is similar to the American Congress.

At the time of the French withdrawal, the major political party was the National Bloc, made up of leading members of landowning families and other well-off individuals. They had been educated in French and Turkish universities or at French- and American-operated colleges in Lebanon and Egypt, and they tended to be a bit snobbish. They had almost no contact with ordinary citizens and seemd uninterested in their needs.

By mid-1947, two other political parties had risen to prominence—the National Party and the People's Party. The National Party represented the industrialists of Damascus, leading businessmen and prominent landowners. The People's Party represented the interests of the merchants and land-lords of Aleppo. It resisted domination by Damascus.

The parties encompassed the country's traditional divisions—the rivalry between Damascus and Aleppo, and between those who favored unity with the Levant (Palestine, Lebanon, and Syria) and those who favored unity with the Fertile Crescent (Iraq, Jordan, and Syria).

But yet another party was evolving, one that eventually would dominate the country. The Ba'ath Party was formed in 1940 by Michel Aflaq and Salah ad Din al Bittar. *Ba'ath* means "resurrection" in Arabic. The party was made up of students, teachers, professionals, and public employees. They comprised Syria's growing middle class. The emergence of a middle class was becoming instrumental in changing Syrian society, because it meant a shift from the traditional wide division between rich and poor toward a more democratic system.

Probably because it was composed of too many idealists and thinkers, the Ba'ath Party didn't have much influence in Syria in its early stages. Its motto was, "Unity, Freedom and Socialism." "Unity" referred to a united Arab nation, one of its guiding principles.

Gradually, the party expanded its membership to include representatives of the lower-middle class. The party saw socialism—government ownership of business—not as an end in itself but as a means of attaining economic and social justice for all.

The Arab superstate envisioned by the Ba'athists was to be based on a secular, rather than a religious, system. This didn't sit well with conservative religious leaders. But the composition of such a superstate was not exactly of pressing interest, since the possibility of such a creation was highly unlikely.

The Ba'athists liked the Marxist concept of a utopian society, but didn't care for communism. Members felt that the communists were too closely allied with the Soviet Union, and the Ba'athists opposed alignment with any of the superpowers.

The fight against Israel in 1948 united the country once again as it dealt with a common enemy. But after the war, the military, angered at what it saw as civilian bungling that lost the war, ousted the civilian government of Shukri al-Quwwatli.

It was a bloodless coup d'etat staged by Colonel Husni Zaim. The takeover was applauded by the press and most members of the public because it seemed to mean a permanent transfer of power from the traditional land-owning elite to a new coalition of young intellectuals, army officers, and the growing middle class.

On August 14, 1949, Zaim was ousted by a military coup engineered by Colonel Sami Hinnawi. He ordered Zaim and his prime minister, Mushin Barazi, arrested and both were executed.

Hinnawi initiated closer ties with the Hashemites in Jordan and Iraq. He was suspected of planning a union between Syria and Iraq, which disturbed certain forces in the army, and he was arrested by Colonel Adib Shishakli, who then proceeded to impose his own military dictatorship on the country.

Street of Shops, Bosra, 1893

Bosra is located approximately 65 miles south of Damascus and is one of the lesser-known large Middle Eastern cities dating from antiquity.

Shishakli formed his own party, the Arab Liberation Movement. In July 1953, Syrians approved a new constitution making Syria a presidential republic rather than a parliamentary one. Shishakli was named president. But his day was almost done. When the Druzes staged a rebellion,

Shishakli declared martial law and bombed the Druzes in their homeland in southern Syria. The patience of his opponents ran out, and Shishakli was ousted in Syria's fourth coup on February 25, 1954.

Shishakli fled to Brazil, where he was assassinated in 1964 by a Druze in retaliation for the earlier bombing.

Meanwhile, the National Party and the People's Party were gradually losing influence. To add to the confusion of political parties vying for power, two more came along—the Syrian Socialist Nationalist Party (SSNP) and the Arab Socialist Party (ASP). In addition, the Syrian Communist Party (SCP) was making itself heard.

The Ba'ath Party was strengthened in 1953 when it merged with the Arab Socialist Party.

The members of these parties did not always engage in polite discussions, as the American political parties do. They tended to get violent. For instance, in April 1955, Colonel Adnan Malik, deputy chief of staff and a leading Ba'athist, was assassinated by a sergeant in the SSNP. This brought about the end of the SSNP, however, as its members were accused of trying to overthrow the government. They either were arrested or fled the country.

In 1957, the Ba'athists entered into a partnership with the Communist Party in an effort to crush conservative opposition, but it backfired. The communists, while small in number, were well-disciplined and determined. They came to dominate the new partnership and the Ba'ath Party started to lose influence.

In order to rid itself of the communists, the Ba'ath Party drafted a bill in 1957 calling for union with Egypt. No one dared oppose the bill because Arab unity was an almost sacred idea. The Ba'athists knew that Egyptian president Gamal Abdel Nasser opposed the concept of political parties and was in the process of persecuting the communists in his own country.

So, Syria and Egypt created the United Arab Republic (UAR) in 1958. But that also backfired.

Akram Hawrani, founder of the Arab Socialist Party, and now head of the Ba'ath Party, was appointed vice president of the new republic. Nasser, of course, was president. The Baathists saw the ascension of Hawrani to a position of power as a sign that they would have a major influence on the new nation. They were wrong.

Syria soon realized it had become a virtual colony of Egypt and many wanted out of the UAR. On September 28, 1961, a military coup did just that, and Syria went back to independence. The country formed a short-lived new government with a constituent assembly composed mostly of members of the conservative People's Party and National Party. People's Party leader Nazim al Qudsi was elected president.

But Syria was plunged into a state of near anarchy in 1961. There were coups and countercoups, street fighting between Nasserites, who wanted to return to union with Egypt, and communists and Ba'athists, as well as battles between rival army factions. The country was in chaos.

This ended in 1963 when a group of senior army officers staged another coup. These army officers, who had used the Ba'ath Party to gain power, soon abandoned its democratic principles and established a military dictatorship. They had organized a secret Military Committee during the merger with Egypt with the aim of seizing power in the UAR. After the country pulled out of the alliance, the officers turned their attention to taking control in Syria.

These officers had no time for Arab unity. They favored Syrian nationalism. Most of the committee members belonged to minority religious groups. The original core of conspirators consisted of three Alawis and two Ismailis. Later, the group was enlarged to 15 members. It then included six Sunni Muslims (the majority sect in Syria), five Alawis, two Druzes, and two Ismailis.

The 1963 coup was seen as a crucial turning point in Syria's history since its independence from France. The focus of Syrian politics shifted to the left, where it remained. Aflaq and Bitar, the Ba'ath Party founders, were expelled from the party. Aflaq was assassinated in Paris in 1980, presumably by Syrian intelligence agents.

In 1967, the country was once again plunged into war with Israel, and the various factions united once more to confront a common enemy.

Ancient Tomb Near Palmyra, 1905

Palmyra was an ancient trading city in south-central Syria. The second and third centuries A.D. were the pinnacle of Palmyran prosperity. In 1980, the United Nations Educational, Scientific, and Cultural Organization (UNESCO) designated the ruins of Palmyra as a World Heritage Site. This photograph was taken by Gertrude Bell, an English traveler, explorer, and prolific writer who made many trips through the Middle Eastern deserts. In 1905, she made a trip to ancient ruins in what is now Syria. These photos were the first taken of these ruins.

7

The
Six-Day
War

amal Abdel Nasser was a victim of his own "big mouth." During his tenure, the Egyptian leader often rattled his country's sabers, only to be unable to sustain his threats and claims. For example, angered because the United States withdrew its offer to finance the Aswan Dam, a project crucial to Egypt's economic development, Nasser nationalized the Suez Canal on July 26, 1956. Britain was furious. It relied on the canal for transportaion of its oil imports. A plan was hatched in which Israel would attack Egypt in the Sinai, then Britain and France would attack Egypt directly.

On October 29, Israel launched its attack with a paratroop drop deep inside the Sinai. Moshe Dayan led the Israeli forces. Within eight days the Israelis drove the Egyptian army out of the desert. Israel claimed it entered Egypt to attack bases used by the *fedayeen* terrorists.

American president Dwight Eisenhower urged Israel to pull out of the Sinai after it took care of the fedayeen bases. But Israeli prime minister Ben-Gurion ignored him. Britain and France then called on Egypt and Israel to pull their forces ten miles from the Suez Canal.

When Egypt refused, as the allies expected it to, Britain and France attacked Egypt on November 6. The attack angered both the United States and the Soviet Union, which was backing Egypt in the fight. In fact, the Soviets threatened to annihilate Israel if it failed to withdraw its forces from the Sinai.

There has been speculation that if the ruthless Joseph Stalin had been alive, it probably would have done just that, possibly provoking World War III.

But Stalin was not alive, and the present leadership of the Soviet Union was mostly just rattling its sabers. However, Eisenhower was furious. He led the pack in the United Nations that demanded Britain and France end their attack. The American president also threatened economic sanctions against Great Britain if it didn't withdraw from Egypt. Eisenhower came to realize that he had been duped by his longtime allies.

One official of the British Foreign Office, referring to the British prime minister's office and residence at Number 10 Downing Street in London, quipped, "It was rather fun to be at Number 10 the night we smashed the Anglo-American alliance."

The war ended quickly after that. Of course, all was eventually forgiven, but for a time the world was on the edge of its seat.

London's *The Sunday Times* wrote that Prime Minister Anthony Eden "was the last prime minister to believe Britain was a great power and the first to confront a crisis which proved beyond doubt that she was not."

Nasser's prestige continued to grow after King Feisal was overthrown in Iraq by Brigadier Karim Qassem on July 14, 1958. Feisal was murdered, along with members of his family and a number of government officials. The revolution resulted from a rising tide of Nasserism in the Arab world.

Then Syria joined Egypt in the United Arab Republic, and Nasser was again riding high.

But in a short time, things started to go very wrong. First, Qassem decided he didn't need Nasser; Iraq would go its own way. In fact, Baghdad radio began insulting the Egyptian president. Then Syria pulled out of the United Arab Republic in September 1961, and Damascus radio started picking on Nasser, too.

Another debacle occurred in September 1962, when Nasser sent a large body of troops into Yemen to rescue the Imam, who had been overthrown in a coup. But that ended in a humiliating disaster when the troops got bogged down and had to return home.

Nasser was also the target of increasing criticism from Arab countries, including Syria, for not taking a hard enough line on Israel. The Syrians were openly hostile to Israel, and the Soviet Union backed them. Thus emerged one of the early confrontations in the Cold War—between the Soviets, backing Syria, and the United States, backing Israel. Something had to give. Nasser found himself deluged with abuse and mockery, to such an extent that his own people were beginning to look at him askance.

The Soviet ambassador to Egypt told Nasser that the Israelis planned to attack Syria on May 13, 1967. That was not true, but it presented Nasser with the need to make a decision. If the Israelis crushed Syria and Nasser did nothing, he would be seen as a traitor to the Arab cause. Nasser put his armed forces on alert and sent them through the Sinai toward Israel's border.

Nasser then announced that he was closing the Straits of Tiran and the Gulf of Aqaba to Israeli shipping, as well as to all ships carrying goods to Israel.

And, again, he had to open his big mouth. "They, the Jews, threaten war; we tell them: Welcome. We are ready for war."

Israeli prime minister Levi Eshkol and his foreign minister, Abba Eban, tried to enlist help from the United States and other powers. He was rebuffed by French president Charles de Gaulle. The British were sympathetic, but made no firm offers of help.

American president Lyndon Johnson spoke of a possible "international naval force" to open the blockades, but that never happened.

The lengthy delay in responding to the Arab threat was met with anger by the Israeli military, and joy by Israel's Arab enemies.

It seemed that Nasser had won a victory and that the Israelis were afraid to fight.

Jordan's King Hussein went to Cairo and placed his armed forces under Egyptian command. The radios of the Arab world stopped attacking each other and concentrated their venom on Israel.

With the appointment of the famous military leader Moshe Dayan as minister for defense, the

Equipage, c. 1912

An equipage is a horse-drawn carriage with attendants. This equipage was
photographed en route to Homs from Palmyra.

Israelis were clearly ready for war.

But Nasser actually was reluctant to go to war with
Israel. He knew the Israelis were tough, but to stop
hostilities, he would have to open the Straits of Tiran
for Israeli shipping, and that he could not do. He was
trapped by his own rhetoric.

The rest of the Arab world was more than ready to
go to war.

The armies of Syria, Egypt, Jordan, and Iraq had
been massing troops along the Israeli border for some

months. Total Arab strength, at least on paper, vastly outnumbered that of Israel. The Arabs had twice as many troops, over three times as many tanks, and more than three times as many combat aircraft.

Taunts and threats from the Arab countries were getting strident. One rabble-rouser, Ahmad Al-Shukairy, then head of the Palestine Liberation Organization, declared, "Those native-born Israelis who will survive the war will be permitted to remain in the country. But I don't think many will survive."

Nasser matched Shukairy's aggressive rhetoric, proclaiming that the very existence of Israel "was in itself an act of aggression."

Syrian defense minister Hafez Assad, future president of Syria, declared, "The army, which has long been preparing itself for the battle and has a finger on the trigger, demands in a single voice that the battle be expedited. . . . The time [has] come to wage the liberation battle. . . . "

Mobs had run amok for days on the streets of Cairo. They called for blood into the microphones and cameras of international television reporters. Egyptian television broadcasts, received in most parts of Israel, cried out for vengeance. Israeli viewers heard the wild chants, and saw the war flags inscribed with black skulls, and the angry faces of the mob screaming for war.

The Arabs were soon to get all the war they wanted.

It was fitting that the coded order for Israel's attack on Egypt was "Nahshonim, action!" Nashon was the leader of the tribe of Judah in the Biblical story of Exodus when the Jews were led out of slavery in Egypt by Moses. Nashon was traditionally believed to have been the first to enter the waters of the Red

Sea after God parted them.

It was June 5, 1967, 7:45 A.M.

Moshe Dayan was in the Israeli Air Force command center, watching the war table before him. When word came that Israeli war planes had made it undetected to Egyptian airfields, the order went out to the armored divisions elsewhere on the nation's threatened borders to start moving.

The Six-Day War, in which Israeli forces defeated the armies of Egypt, Jordan, and Syria in less than a week, had begun.

Israeli planes pounced on Egyptian airfields, catching most of the planes on the ground. Between 7:14 A.M. and 8:55 A.M., 11 Egyptian airfields were attacked and 197 Egyptian aircrafts were destroyed, 189 on the ground and 8 in dogfights in the air. Six airfields were completely knocked out, four in Sinai and two west of the Suez Canal, and sixteen radar stations were put out of action.

That was only the first wave. In the second wave, 164 planes attacked 14 air bases and destroyed 107 more Egyptian aircraft. The Israelis lost eleven pilots, six killed, two taken prisoner, and three wounded. Nine planes were lost.

The Syrian, Jordanian, and Iraqi air forces launched their attacks on Israel unaware of the destruction of the Egyptian aircraft. Twelve Russian-made MiG-17s took off from Damascus at 11:50 A.M. Two of them attacked Kibbutz Degania, where Dayan had grown up, setting fire to a silo and a poultry run. The Syrian planes then went on to attack—and miss—an Israeli stronghold at Bet Yerach, on the Sea of Galilee, and a dam on the Jordan River.

Three other MiGs attacked an airfield in the

Jezreel Valley, and one was brought down by antiaircraft guns. Another flight of three mistakenly set a haystack and a granary on fire near Kibbutz Ein Hamifratz in the belief that they were bombing Haifa oil refineries.

The rest of the planes strafed and rocketed a convalescent home at Kfar Hahoresh, near Nazareth, damaging buildings and wounding one Jew and one Arab.

Syria lost almost 50 percent of its air force—53 planes destroyed out of a total of 112—in 82 Israeli attack sorties on the Syrian air bases of Damir, Damascus, Seikal, Marjarial, and T-4.

Other countries did equally poorly in the air. Jordanian planes took off at noon and attacked the coastal resort of Netanya and the Kfar Syrkin airfield near Petach Tikvah. They destroyed only a Nord transport plane on the ground at Kfar Syrkin.

Two hours later three Iraqi planes fired rockets in the direction of the settlement at Nahalal, no doubt believing it was the Ramat David airfield. They caused no damage and returned to Iraq.

Jordan and Iraq paid dearly for these attacks. Israeli planes destroyed the entire Jordanian air force of 28 planes in attacks on the two Jordanian air bases of Mafrak and Amman. Iraq lost ten planes in a three-sortie attack on one field, called 3-H.

In Egypt, Cairo Radio was bragging that the Egyptian Air Force had shot down 40 Israeli planes. There was no truth to that, of course, but it was typical of the way the Egyptians were deluding themselves that they were having an easy time with the Israeli forces. In reality, they were being crushed.

Sinai was cleared of Egyptian forces in fierce fighting. Israeli troops smashed their way to the Suez Canal.

"After four days of bloody battle, failure, and traumatic shock experienced by both his soldiers in the field and by their superiors—political as well as military —Nasser accepted the cease-fire," Dayan wrote in his autobiography.

Meanwhile, Israeli forces were dealing with King Hussein's Jordanian army at the divided city of Jerusalem. The Jordanians were soon out of the war and Israel had control of Jerusalem for the first time since it was divided after the 1948 war.

The Israelis were now able to turn their full attention to its last remaining enemy—Syria.

Syria had resisted Egypt's plea that it launch an all-out attack on Israel. Except for a few bombing sorties that didn't really hit anything, the Syrians set up a defensive strategy with occasional forays into Israel territory. It cancelled what had been called "Operation Nasser" in favor of "Operation *Jihad* (Holy War)," and, along with its brief and generally unsuccesful attacks across the border, concentrated on shelling a northern kibbutz and army camps.

On June 9, Israeli troops and armor attacked the Syrian positions on the border. It was then that the Israelis captured the Golan Heights. The fight for Golan was tough for Israel because the Syrians commanded the high ground and were able to fire down on the advancing Israelis. But the Israeli troops were able to gain command of the Syrian positions by nightfall.

Israeli air support also helped to turn the tide of battle. In the northern part of Golan, Syrians held out heroically against the enemy. Dayan said, "The Syrian force at Zaoura put up a stubborn defense and fought well. But it was soon overcome."

Another difficult battle took place at Tel Faher, and again Syrian troops fought fiercely. But on Saturday, June 10, advancing Israelis found the Syrian positions empty. The Syrians had abandoned them during the night, leaving antitank guns and heavy and light machine guns behind.

The Syrians retreated toward Damascus, 40 miles away. Fearing that the Israelis would march on the capital, the government instructed its United Nations delegates to urge the Security Council to adopt a cease-fire resolution.

The Israelis set up a frontier between them and the Syrians that included a large piece of Syrian territory. The Israelis now commanded the high ground, with a clear view of the plain stretching toward Damascus.

"In their mind's eye," Dayan wrote of the Syrians, "they would see us getting into our tanks and galloping on to Damascus whenever the fancy should take us. This may have been thought a flight of Oriental fantasy, but anyone going up to the Golan Heights and seeing the vast plain stretching away toward Damascus could hardly rule out such a possibility."

Among those made nervous by that possibility were the Soviets. In fact, the Soviets warned the United States that if the U.S. did not stop the Israeli advance, the Soviets would intervene on behalf of the Syrians.

Diplomatic cables flashed around the world. The Israelis told the United States that they had no intention of advancing any further. Their only intention, they said, was to put their settlements out of artillery range.

In the swift war, the Israelis captured the Sinai Peninsula from Egypt, occupied the east bank of the Suez Canal, shutting it down; and took the West Bank and Jerusalem from Jordan and the Golan Heights from Syria.

Emotionally, the capture of the Old City of Jerusalem was the high point of the war for Israel. Jews were now able to visit and pray at the Western Wall of Herod's Temple. They had been unable to visit this holy shrine while it was held by the Jordanians.

But the occupation by Israel of Egyptian and Syrian territories sowed the seeds for future violence among those countries. For the Syrians, the loss of Golan was to become a sore point for decades to come; it would influence all of their decisions about relations with Israel, and cause ceaseless upheaval in their own country.

Inside the English Consul's House, Damascus, c. 1890

8
A Region Divided

O ne couldn't keep track of the leaders of the Syrian government in the 1960s without a scorecard. But there was no scorecard available.

Just as one man or faction attained power, another man or faction shoved them out the door. Nevertheless, the changes of government, however abrupt, were usually accomplished without the shedding of blood—but not always.

Just before the Six-Day War, there were frequent changes of government because of a struggle that began in 1964 between the centrist and leftist wings of the dominant Ba'ath Party. (Left-wingers tended to be more radically socialist and the right-wingers more conservative. The centrists were, of course, in the middle. The political terms of "left" and "right" stemmed from the seating arrangements in the French National Assembly of 1789.)

On July 17 and 18, 1963, some 2,000 Syrian Nasserites—supporters of the president of Egypt—attempted a coup. It was crushed by the military after heavy fighting in Damascus. Major General Amin al Hafiz, commander in chief of the armed forces, emerged as the country's newest strongman.

This was the first time that a coup or coup attempt had led to violence and loss of life. On July 19, justice for the rebels was swift. Eight army officers and twelve civilians involved in the uprising were convicted in summary trials before revolutionary security courts and executed by firing squads the same day.

Hafiz later became prime minister and held a number of other government posts before he was ousted in another bloody coup on February 23, 1966. That coup was engineered by two Ba'athist generals, Salah al Jadid and Hafez al Assad, both members of the Muslim Alawi sect.

Hafiz, wounded in the fighting, was arrested and jailed. Assad, the future president of Syria, was named minister of defense, the post he held when the Six-Day War broke out.

On September 8, 1966, a military countercoup led by a Druze, Salim Hatum, failed when Assad threatened to send the air force after Hatum's forces. Hatum and his associates fled to Jordan, but he came back in June 1967, saying he wanted to fight against Israel. He was shot.

The traumatic defeat in the Six-Day War discredited the radical socialist regimes of both Nasser's Egypt and Ba'athist Syria. As a result, the defeat had the effect of strengthening the hands of the moderates and rightists in the Ba'ath Party and became the catalyst for Assad's rise to power.

Meanwhile, the great powers continued to view activities in the Middle East through the prism of the Cold War. Both the United States and the Soviet Union tended to see every major crisis there as the result of a sinister plot by the other side to gain power and influence in the region.

In the United States, there was a continuing debate between the "globalists" and the "regionalists" in dealing with the Middle East. The globalists regarded the conflicts as a struggle for supremacy between the United States and the Soviet Union. The regionalists saw the problems as more local and tried to figure out how the United States could help solve them.

The State of Israel was at the core of the debate. The globalists viewed Israel as an asset because it countered Soviet influence on the Arab countries. The regionalists tended to see Israel as a liability, contending that supporting Israel opened the door to Soviet intervention on the side of the Arabs and prevented America from having constructive dealings with the Arabs.

The Israel-first school of thought dominated American policy after the 1967 war. For one thing, Americans, both Jews and non-Jews, admired the Israelis. They liked their pioneering spirit, because it was that same spirit that built America. They also admired their courage, their fighting abilities, and their democratic ways in a region that did not see much democracy.

In addition, American politicians had to deal with the powerful Israeli lobby on its own soil and the equally potent and usually unified Jewish vote.

The first meeting of the Arab states after the Six-Day War occurred from August 19 to September 1, 1967, at Khartoum. The meeting produced the famous "three no's"— no peace with Israel, no recognition of Israel, and no negotiations with Israel concerning any Palestinian territory.

On November 22, 1967, the United Nations asserted itself in the Middle East with Security Council Resolution 242, which called for Israel to withdraw its armed forces "from territories occupied in the recent conflict." It called on the Arabs to end their belligerence and recognize Israel's right to

Motor Trolley Used Between Aleppo and the Euphrates River, c. 1912

This eight-passenger omnibus was driven by a four-horsepower single-cylinder gasoline engine. Specially designed metal wheels allowed the vehicle to operate on tracks. By 1905, a railroad line was completed from Constantinople to Beirut. Aleppo was a rail stop on this line, and many tourists took this motor trolley ride to see the Euphrates River. Note the men are wearing the traditional *fez* or Turkish hat.

live peacefully within secure and recognized boundaries.

The resolution was subject to different interpretations. The Arabs thought it meant that the Israelis should immediately pull out of the territories it had taken in the Six-Day War. To the Israelis, the resolution meant negotiations should begin, leading to formal peace treaties that included establishing those "secure and recognized boundaries."

The American government interpreted it to mean there should be minor adjustments in the western frontier of the West Bank, demilitarization measures in the Sinai and the Golan Heights, and a fresh look at the status of Jerusalem.

United States president Richard M. Nixon and his national security adviser, Henry Kissinger, were globalists. Their policy was simply to explore ways to expel the Soviet Union from the Middle East. This would not involve committing troops, as in the conflict in Vietnam, but supporting local allies. Therefore, America offered Israel diplomatic support, economic assistance, and arms on an ever-growing scale.

In 1969, another crisis occurred that would test the patience of both globalists and regionalists. Nasser, frustrated by the standstill on dealing with the problem of Israel, launched what became known as the "War of Attrition."

This so-called "war" was at first a duel of artillery fire across the Suez Canal. Egypt hoped to dislodge the Israelis from the Sinai. The Israelis responded by bombing Egypt. They believed they would have American support because the War of Attrition would gradually bleed Israel to death.

Nasser dashed off to Moscow to get Soviet help. He demanded surface-to-air missiles and Russian crews to operate them. To Soviet premier Leonid Brezhnev, he said, "I am a leader who is bombed every day in his own country, whose army is exposed and whose people are naked. I have the courage to tell our people the unfortunate truth—that, whether they like it or not, the Americans are masters of the world."

Hearing this, the Soviets agreed to give Nasser everything he asked for, and more.

On July 30, Israeli fighters shot down four Soviet planes near the Suez Canal. The next day, the government of Israel agreed to accept a cease-fire and the application of the United Nations' Resolution 242.

Golda Meir, then prime minister of Israel, "had at last jammed on the brakes, very near to the edge of the cliff," writes Conor Cruise O'Brien in his book, *The Siege.*

But the Golda Meir government dragged its feet in negotiating a peace with Egypt. Nasser died and Anwar Sadat took over. Sadat was more amenable to negotiations than his hot-headed predecessor. But, still, no progress was made, and it became increasingly clear that more bloodshed was in store for the region.

Meanwhile, Syria was highly critical of Jordan and Lebanon for their efforts to control Palestinian guerrillas in their territories. But, at the same time, the Syrians kept a tight lid on terrorist activities in their own country. They were especially watchful of the radical *As Saiqa* (Thunderbolt). *As Saiqa* was not allowed to use Syria as a base for attacks on Israel for fear of Israeli reprisals.

In September 1970, the Jordanian army launched attacks on camps on Jordanian soil belonging to the radical Palestine Liberation Organization (PLO) and on Palestinian refugee camps that were under the control of PLO units near Amman. This offensive became known to the PLO as "Black September."

Syria sent about 200 tanks to aid the PLO forces. The armored vehicles were supposed to have been supplied by the Palestine Liberation Army (PLA), but basically they were Syrian tanks.

Iraqi troops gathered on the Jordanian border, but did not enter the country.

The world was so alarmed by these activities that the United States sent its Sixth Fleet to the eastern Mediterranean. As part of the Cold War mentality of the day, the United States was convinced that the Soviet Union was behind the crisis.

The Syrian tanks came under heavy fire by Jordanian troops and war planes and were forced to withdraw.

This failure of the Syrian intervention could be traced back to the same domestic political disagreements within the Baath leadership that were disrupting the country internally. The Jadid faction of the party wanted full support of the PLO in Jordan and participation in its activities. But Assad and his associates opposed such action. Assad had refused to send his air force to support the tanks in Jordan, primarily because he feared a devastating attack from Israel.

On November 13, 1970, Jadid was out. Army units

arrested him and his associates. Three days later the regional command of the Ba'ath Party issued a statement saying the change that had occurred was merely a transfer of power within the party. A new party congress was to be convened to reorganize the party; a national front government was to be organized under the new Ba'athist leadership, and a people's council, or legislature, was to be formed. The statement also affirmed continued support for the Palestinian cause.

Three days after that, Ahmad al Khatib was named acting chief of staff and Assad prime minister and minister of defense. Assad also claimed the change in government was not a coup. He called it a "correction movement."

So, by the end of the 1960s, Syria was at odds with its Arab neighbors. The Ba'athist Party in Syria was fighting with the Ba'athist Party in Iraq. The Syrians felt the Iraqi Ba'athists were trying to interfere with the party in Syria.

Syria and Jordan were smarting over their disputes dealing with the Palestinian Liberation Organization. There was still anger at the Egyptians for the continuing efforts of the Nasserites to influence Syrian policy. Nasser's dream had always been of a Pan-Arab nation dominated by Egypt. The Syrians didn't like that idea at all.

Syria was angry at the Western powers, especially the United States, for their continued support of the hated Israelis. And even the Soviets, who had supplied Syria with arms and other goods, were looked at with suspicion. Syrians didn't like to be too cozy with powerful nations that could dominate them.

And, of course, the Syrians were still furious at the Israelis for their occupation of the Golan Heights. The continuing hatred of the Israelis led the Syrians to the ill-fated decision to join Egypt in another attack on Israel.

Disaster loomed.

Square and Pillar, 1908

Today, this is Marjeh Square, which used to be the Damascus city center during the French Mandate (1922–45) and the terminus for the tram lines. The large column commemorates the first telegraph link between Damascus and Mecca.

The second and third buildings (left to right) were the headquarters of the Hejaz Railroad Company. The railroad station (left building) was built by the Ottomans to transport pilgrims from Damascus to Medina.

The Yom Kippur War and Lebanon Conflicts

Yom Kippur is the holiest day in the Jewish calendar. It is a day of fasting and prayer for forgiveness of sins committed during the year. Jews gather in synagogues on the eve of Yom Kippur when the fast begins, and return the following morning to continue confessing, doing penance, and praying for forgiveness.

The Arab nations thought there would be no better time to attack Israel.

The Yom Kippur War began at 2 P.M. on October 6, 1973. Egyptian and Syrian forces attacked at the same time, catching the Israelis by surprise for another war.

The Israelis were not totally unprepared, however. On the Syrian front they had a fighting force of some 180 tanks, 11 artillery batteries, and 5,000 men. On the Egyptian front they had about 275 tanks, 12 artillery batteries, and 8,500 men.

The Israelis were informed that the United States had sent a message to Egypt demanding to know what its intentions were. The United States contacted Syria indirectly, through the Soviet Union. No response came from either country.

Both Egypt and Syria had informed the Soviets of their intentions and the Soviets made no effort to change their minds.

Syrian aircraft had crossed Israeli air space and Egyptian troops were crossing the Suez Canal on rafts. The Soviets had been equipping and training the armies of both Egypt and Syria for some time. A new shipment of 15 batteries of Russian-made SA-6 (surface-to-air) missiles had been dispatched to Syria and ten to Egypt. Syria also received Frog-7 surface-to-surface missiles with a range of 40 miles.

In addition, the Soviets had provided both countries with about 500 T-62 tanks, as well as such antitank weapons as Sagger missiles, RPGs (rocket-propelled grenades) and other arms.

The Egyptian offensive opened with an air attack accompanied by an artillery barrage against Israeli forces on the east bank of the Suez Canal. Some 2,000 Egyptian guns opened up along the entire front. In the first minute of the attack, 10,500 shells from medium and heavy artillery and medium and heavy mortars fell on Israeli positions. That amounted to 175 shells per second.

The Frogs—the surface-to-surface missiles—opened up. Tanks rolled up to ramps prepared on the sand ramparts of the canal and began firing. "Over 3,000 tons of concentrated destruction were launched against a handful of Israeli fortifications in a barrage that turned the east bank of the Suez Canal into an inferno in 53 minutes," one observer wrote.

After the shelling, 8,000 Egyptian infantrymen crossed the canal. Further waves followed. They were opposed by 436 Israeli soldiers along the 110-mile length of the Suez Canal.

On the northern front, the Syrians launched a similarly devastating attack. Two Israeli brigades came under attack from three Syrian divisions—1,100 tanks against 157 tanks. After 22 hours of fighting, 90 percent of the officers of the Israeli brigades and most of the men were either killed or wounded.

On October 7, the Egyptian Seventh Division had crossed the Suez Canal with all its forces.

A counterattack by the Israelis the next day failed. In three days, Israel had lost 50 aircraft and hundreds of tanks.

Three days later, Golda Meir was calling for a cease-fire that would give the Egyptians the territory they had conquered. But by that time, the Israelis had called up their reserves and rallied their armies from the Yom Kippur break and were ready to fight back.

The Israelis concentrated their attack on the Syrians on the northern front. By October 10, the Syrians had been driven out of all the territory they had grabbed in the opening days of the war.

The next day, Israeli forces invaded Syria. They seemed to be heading for Damascus. This alarmed the Soviets and they began a massive airlift of armaments to Cairo and Damascus. The United States responded with an equally massive airlift of armaments to Israel. Another East–West confrontation was on.

On Sunday morning, October 8, Egyptian armored forces began an offensive in the Sinai. The Israelis won it decisively, knocking out 264 Egyptian tanks and losing only ten tanks themselves.

After the tank battle, the Egyptians retreated to the Suez Canal. Israeli forces under the command of General Ariel Sharon stormed across the canal, destroying missile bases and trapping the Egyptian Third Army.

Negotiations had gotten underway between the Americans and the Soviets for a cease-fire that would be ordered by the United Nations. But fighting started up again when Israeli forces surrounded the Egyptian Third Army and threatened to annihilate it or starve it out. The result was the most serious confrontation between the United States and the Soviet Union since the Cuban Missile Crisis of 1962. The Soviets made it clear they would not put up with the destruction of Egypt's Third Army, and that they would take action to prevent it.

The United States put its own military on alert.

But the confrontation ended when Israel agreed to the cease-fire on October 25, 1973. Thus, the Yom Kippur War had ended in a stalemate, leaving no one satisfied and laying the groundwork for future conflict between Israel and its Arab neighbors.

One of the more significant of these conflicts took place in Lebanon.

In 1975, civil war broke out in Lebanon between Christians and Muslims, with participation by the Palestine Liberation Organization. Both Israel and Syria considered intervening. Syrian president Hafez Assad, who had taken over Syria in 1970, knew that a takeover of Lebanon by Muslim forces and the PLO would invite an Israeli attempt to occupy the country.

Syria and Lebanon had a special relationship going back centuries. Syria considered Lebanon part of "Greater Syria"

Syrian Tanks in Lebanon, 1976

Children pose for a photograph with the crew of a Syrian T-54 tank in Beirut, Lebanon, in 1976. The Syrian army was part of the Arab peacekeeping force attempting to bring an end to Lebanon's 19-month civil war.

and had considerable influence in the country. And neither the United States nor Israel had any objections to Syrian intervention in Lebanon.

So, in January 1976, a detachment of 50 Syrian officers was sent to Beirut to help enforce one of a series of cease-fires among the combatants. On March 16, Syria ordered

Syrian-backed units of the Palestine Liberation Army (the standing army of the PLO) to stop leftist Muslim forces from attacking the palace of the country's Christian president, Sulayman Franjiyah.

The Syrian presence in Lebanon grew rapidly. On April 9, about 3,000 Syrian regular troops entered the country. In May, the Lebanese Parliament elected a new, Syrian-backed Christian president, Elias Sarkis. By the fall, more than 22,000 Syrian troops were in Lebanon.

In June 1978, Christian militamen assassinated Christian leader Tony Franjiyah, a son of the fomer president and Syria's staunchest ally in Lebanon. That deed provoked the Syrians into, more or less, switching sides. They began massive artillery barrages on Christian territory in East Beirut.

The Syrians were roundly criticized for attacks that were causing the deaths of innocent civilians. Nevertheless, Syrian troops remained in Lebanon.

In June 1982, Israel and Syria clashed when the Israelis invaded Lebanon to knock out PLO bases that had been used to launch terrorist attacks on Israel. The Israelis at the same time fired on the missile bases Syria had set up in Lebanon's Bekka Valley. On June 9, the Israeli air force attacked the Syrian air-defense system, knocking out 17 SAM-6, SAM-3, and SAM-2 batteries. In a fierce air battle, Israeli planes shot down 25 Syrian planes, without a loss to Israel. Israeli troops then marched into Beirut.

The Syrian and PLO forces were trapped in West Beirut, and the Israelis began shelling them. By August 1982, the Palestinians and Syrians were ready to give up. More than 10,000 men belonging to various PLO units and 4,000 Syrian troops were allowed to pull out.

By this time, Israel and Egypt had signed a peace treaty—on March 27, 1979, in Washington—ending 31 years of war. The treaty resulted from the famous Camp David negotiations organized by U.S. president Jimmy

Carter. Carter had brought Egyptian president Anwar Sadat and Israeli prime minister Menachem Begin together at the presidential retreat in Maryland. After 13 days of tough negotiations, the two sides agreed to certain conditions: Israel would withdraw from Sinai, and relations between the two countries would be normalized. In addition, the United States agreed to continue its support and to provide economic help as needed.

Syria blamed the disaster of Lebanon on what it saw as Egypt's defection from the Arab cause by signing a treaty with Israel. The fact was that once Egypt had withdrawn from the Arab coalition, no combination of the other Arab states was strong enough to fight Israel.

On August 23, 1982, while the PLO and Syrians were evacuating West Beirut, Bashir Gemayel, a Maronite Christian and leader of the Lebanese Christian Phalangists Party, was elected president of Lebanon. The Syrians were angered. The Damascus newspaper *al-Ba'ath* accused Bashir of treason, and declared that the "day of judgment [was] near."

It was right. On September 14. 1982, Bashir was killed by a bomb detonated at a party headquarters building in West Beirut. In Damascus, *al-Ba'ath* praised the killing. The suspect arrested in the bombing, Habib Shaartouni, turned out to be a member of the Syrian Social Nationalist Party.

The Israeli reaction was to occupy West Beirut "to prevent any possible incident and to secure quiet."

The Israelis then made the disastrous decision to let the Christian Phalangists into Palestinian refugee camps at Sabra and Chatila to clear out any terrorists. The Phalangists proceeded to slaughter men, women, and children in revenge for Bashir's murder. It took them two days to massacre several hundred people.

The Israelis were accused of complicity in the slaughter. But in denying any responsibility, Begin told a reporter,

"Goyim kill goyim, and they immediately come to hang the Jews."

Bashir's brother, Amin, was elected president of Lebanon.

The new American president, Ronald Reagan, had an ambitious plan for Lebanon. He wanted both Israel and Syria out of the country. Israel pulled out of its positions in the Druze area of the Shouf mountains, but as soon as it left, the Druzes attacked the Christians there and massacred an estimated 17,000 people in Christian villages.

Alarmed by the violence, Reagan sent U.S. Marines into Lebanon to help keep order. His position on the Syrians, whose troops remained in Lebanon, was, as he put it, to keep them "on the outside looking in."

In September, marine artillery and the guns of the Sixth Fleet were used to support Lebanese government troops against the rebels. But on October 23, 1983, terrorists driving trucks loaded with explosives penetrated the perimeter of the marine barracks in Beirut. The blasts killed 241 marines. It was assumed that Syria was behind the attack.

On December 3, U.S. aircraft attacked Syrian antiaircraft positions. The United States itched to do more damage to Syria in retaliation for the attack, but it soon realized its options were limited. Reagan pulled the marines out of Lebanon in February 1984.

Before the disaster, an Israeli commentator had noted, "After much bloodshed among Lebanese, Syrians, Palestinians, and Israelis, the U.S., without firing a shot, became the dominant power in an area previously ruled by two close allies of the Soviet Union."

But the U.S. no longer wanted to accept that role. It had suffered too much, and the American public didn't want to see any more body bags coming home.

Three minutes after the last marine left the beach in Beirut on February 26, the U.S. seashore base was taken over by gunmen of the Shia Muslim Amal movement, linked to

Syria and Iran. Some had little pictures of the Iranian religious leader, Ayatollah Khomeini, around their necks.

The Israelis were satisfied that they had expelled the PLO from Beirut and saw no reason for further conflict. The Syrians remained in parts of the country, and continued to exert its controlling interest in Lebanon.

A sort of uneasy peace descended on the region.

Golan Heights Land Mines

A sign warns of land mines, planted by both Israeli and Syrian troops, in outlying fields near the Syrian-Israeli border in the Golan Heights. The International Campaign to Ban Land Mines estimates that as of 2000 there were 76 minefields planted across the Golan Heights.

10
The
Strongman

The man who would run Syria longer than any other leader in modern Syrian history was born October 6, 1930, in the village of Qardaha, a farming community of mud and stone dwellings.

Hafez Assad was a quiet, gangly boy who showed an early interest in politics. He hated the French, who then occupied Syria with a League of Nations mandate. He developed an interest in Arab nationalism even as a child. He was a member of the Alawi Muslim sect in a country where the Sunni Muslims were in the majority.

Assad was fortunate; his father was one of the few literate

people in the village and encouraged his son's studies. Hafez was elected president of the Union of Syrian Students in 1951. A year later, he entered the Syrian Military Academy at Homs. After graduation, he joined the elite air force and became a fighter pilot. He was named the best pilot in his class at an air training school in Aleppo. His experience as a pilot gave him a lifelong appreciation of the importance of aircraft in combat.

While Syria was part of the United Arab Republic with Egypt from 1958 to 1961, Assad found himself on the outside looking in. He bided his time, and when he saw an opportunity to form a military committee of Syrian officers serving in Egypt, he had found his calling.

In 1963, the committee helped bring the Ba'ath Party into power in a bloodless coup d'etat. Assad held the rank of major general and was named air force commander. After another coup in 1966, he was named defense minister. In 1970, still another coup elevated him to prime minister. He was elected president for a seven-year term in 1971, and was regularly and easily reelected after that. The magazine *The Economist* once called the Syrian government under Assad "a family and tribal clique within a military junta." (A junta is a group of people who get together to run a country, usually following a revolution.)

Assad was a soft-spoken man with a high forehead and small mustache. He neither drank alcohol nor smoked, and did not eat meat. He was a workaholic, spending long hours doing government work. He had practically no social life.

His great hero was the Kurdish warrior Salah al-Din, known as Saladin, who defeated the Crusaders. He had a picture of Saladin on his office wall.

Assad made efforts to rebuild his economically depressed country and rid the government of long-entrenched corruption. He built roads, schools, hospitals, and low-cost housing.

But the major goal of his life was to take revenge on the Israelis for Syria's humiliating defeat in the 1967 Six-Day War.

He was particularly passionate about reclaiming the Golan Heights, lost to Israel in that war. He saw Israeli occupation of the strategically important high ground as a dagger aimed at Syria's heart. This passion colored all of his dealings with Israel, and hindered any chance of a peace treaty with the hated enemy.

In the 1973 Yom Kippur War, Syria managed to reclaim a slice of territory in Golan. The amount of territory was insignificant from a strategic point of view. Nevertheless, Assad saw this as a victory and personally raised the Syrian flag there.

After the Soviet Union's demise in 1991, Syria no longer had the backing of its old ally. So, Assad reluctantly entered into negotiations with Israel on a possible peace treaty. Talks didn't get very far because of Assad's determination to make the return of the Golan Heights a requirement for peace.

After Assad's death on June 10, 2000, the world waited to see what his son and successor, Bashar, would do.

Bashar vowed to reform an economy saddled with archaic laws, backward technology, a stifling bureaucracy, and rampant corruption. He approved new laws to establish private banks, and introduced measures to set up a stock market and private universities and to liberalize the currency system.

The Washington Post, in an article on March 27, 2001, used the example of a state-owned cookie factory in

Damascus to illustrate what Bashar faced in trying to change the Syrian economy.

> [A]t the Ghraoui Biscuit Co., 90 workers churn out their notoriously unpopular tea biscuits, even though the plant's market has dwindled to a few state-owned stores, the workweek has shrunk to four days, and Syrian officials say a portion of the goods go home with the employees.

In most capital societies, the plant would have been put out of business long ago. But closing it would have been virtually impossible in Syria. Syrians believe the system that keeps such unprofitable and inefficient businesses going is crucial to social harmony. Keeping it open, however, meant giving in to a system that had corroded the country's economy and elevated corruption and cronyism to the normal way of conducting business.

Bashar was handed a country that his father had allowed to drift toward obsolescence. But how could he create a private banking system where there were no bankers? How could he install modern management without trained managers, and how could he shed assets like the crumbling cookie factory without alienating the political allies he needed to stay in power?

Some things hadn't changed in a Syria used to firm control from the top. One day in 2001, a man named Nizar Nayyouf was yanked out of his car in broad daylight by police, who threw a sack over his head and whisked him away.

Apparently, security forces had acted on their own, as they were accustomed to doing. Only an order from the top secured Nayyouf's release. The government then tried to say the abduction had never taken place.

Actually, the fact that Nayyouf, whose "crime" was not revealed, survived the abduction without being tortured or killed, a frequent occurrence in the Hafez Assad era, indicated that things might be less repressive under Bashar.

However, Bashar continued his father's policy of blasting Israel. In March 2001, he said Israeli society is "more racist than the Nazis."

And when Pope John Paul II arrived in Damascus in May 2001, he found himself standing silently by as Bashar launched into a tirade against the Jews, calling them betrayers of Jesus. Asked why the Pope hadn't responded to the Syrian, all the Vatican could say was that the Pope and the Catholic Church are strongly opposed to anti-Semitism.

Then in January 2002, Syria's deputy United Nations ambassador, Fayssal Mekdad, used the occasion of Syria's first speech as a new member of the U.N. Security Council to accuse Israel of "state terrorism" against the Palestinians.

He compared recent Israeli actions against Palestinians in the Rafah refugee camp in Gaza, where Israeli tanks demolished houses of suspected terrorists, to the devastation of the World Trade Center on September 11, 2001.

A U.S. official called the statement "extremely unfortunate, unhelpful and offensive."

It was unlikely that Mekdad made his remarks without clearance from Bashar Assad. This led to speculation that as much as Assad wanted to make changes in his country, he still had to appease those who wanted to continue the hard line against Israel.

For example, the issue of terrorism and Syria's role in fostering or combating it has become a significant issue for the new regime. The story of Khalid al-Shami helps to illustrate this point.

Bashar Assad and Pope John Paul II, 2001

Syrian president Bashar Assad escorts Pope John Paul II as he arrives at Damascus Airport in May 2001. Assad took the opportunity to put the blame for Israeli-Palestinian violence on Israel, as had his famous father.

Al-Shami had spent 20 years in prison for being a ranking member of the Muslim Brotherhood, a fundamentalist Islamic movement, which was ruthlessly suppressed in 1982 by Syrian president Hafez Assad.

Now, with Assad dead and his son, Bashar, in control, Shami was released from prison in December 2001.

He was lost in a Damascus he didn't recognize.

"I couldn't find my house because everything had changed," he told a *New York Times* reporter. "I didn't know where I was."

He checked into a hotel after convincing the manager that the dark-haired, 40-year-old man on his expired driver's license and passport was indeed he.

Shami considered himself lucky not only to be free, but to be alive.

Human rights groups condemned the violent suppression of the Muslim Brotherhood in the city of Hama, Syria as an enormous atrocity. At least 10,000 people were killed by bullets, bombs, and collapsing buildings. It took 27 days to complete the destruction of Hama.

Amnesty International estimates 25,000 were killed.

After the soldiers were finished slaughtering the populace, the bulldozers came in and leveled whole blocks of buildings, not bothering to check first to see if any were still inhabited.

But 20 years later, the people of Hama applauded the attacks on the rebellious sect. There was a feeling that the Assad government had done the right thing.

The Apamee Cham Palace Hotel was built on the site where Muslim Brotherhood members were executed. A bartender there told a reporter for *The San Francisco Chronicle*, "They were against the nature of Syria. They're not cultured. They're not civilized."

A 30-foot statue of Hafez Assad now stands in the town.

Assad had some reason to be worried about the brotherhood. Just four months before his crackdown, Islamic extremists had assassinated Egyptian president Anwar Sadat. And Assad was afraid the same thing could happen to him.

Ever since Assad had become president of Syria, he did not hesitate to use force against his opponents. And there was no doubt that he employed terrorists, who trained in camps on his territory, to take care of enemies.

Since 1979, Syria has been on the United States' list of countries that support terrorists. The U.S. State Department claimed Syria provided the Abu Nidal terrorist organization logistical support and permission to operate facilities in Damascus. Reports in the 1980s said Syria provided training camps for Middle Eastern and international terrorists. There were five training bases near Damascus and some 20 other training facilities elsewhere in the country, according to the reports.

U.S. News & World Report wrote in 1986 that large numbers of international terrorists known to Western intelligence agencies had turned up in Damascus in the early 1980s. Even Western European terrorists were reported to have trained in Syria and Lebanon. They included such unrelated groups as the Red Army Faction, also known as the Baader Meinhof Gang, of Germany; the Armenian Secret Army for the Liberation of Armenia; the Japanese Red Army; the Kurdish Labor Party; the Pakistani Az Zulifkar; and the Tamil United Liberation Front, as well as groups from Sri Lanka, the Philippines, Oman, Somalia, and other countries.

Middle East analysts found that Syrian intelligence services used terrorist organizations to further the country's interests and to eliminate opposition. The Syrians also used terrorists as surrogates to avoid direct blame, analysts said. Some operated outside the country.

Jordanian officials accused Syria of being behind the assassination of two Jordanian diplomats in Athens and Madrid, and of wounding two others in India and Italy. PLO leaders accused Syria of the assassination of Said Sayil, also known as Abu Walid, Yasir Arafat's chief of staff.

In the U.S. Department of State's *Patterns of Global Terrorism: 1983,* it was reported that several attacks by members of the Abu Nidal organization were traced to Syrian opposition to the pro-Arafat Fatah faction of the PLO.

The attacks included the murder of Issam Sartqwi, a PLO observer at the International Conference of Socialists in Portugal. The same report charged Syria with encouraging the radical Shia Lebanese group Islamic Jihad to carry out the 1983 suicide bombing attacks against the U.S. Embassy and the marine barracks in Beirut.

Spotted in Damascus were Abu Musa, leader of a radical PLO faction who had nearly succeeded in taking the Palestinian leadership from Yasir Arafat, and Habib Tanyus Shartuni, who was said to have admitted killing Lebanese president Bashir Gemayel in 1982, touching off the Syrian invasion of Lebanon.

However, in 1987, Assad closed Abu Nidal's office in Damascus, and worked to win the release of French and U.S. hostages held by terrorist groups. In that year, also, Assad resumed normal diplomatic relations with the United States. One of the reasons that Assad wanted to appease the United States was that Syria's former sponsor, the Soviet Union, was nearing collapse.

In 1990, when Iraq suddenly invaded Kuwait, President George Bush rounded up a number of other countries, including Arab nations, to help defeat Iraqi dictator Saddam Hussein. Assad contributed an armored division to the multinational "Desert Storm" force that liberated Kuwait.

That sent his stock up with Western countries. But he had taken advantage of the world's focus on the Persian Gulf to move the Syrian army deeper into Lebanon. The Israelis finally evacuated Lebanon in May 2000, leaving the country to Syria, which installed a pro-Syrian government.

Assad was not ready to give up his demand that Israel return what he considered to be Syrian property. In an interview with *The Washington Post*, Assad declared, "If Israel is not going to quit the occupied land, why then should we want peace? No people can accept anything as a substitute for their land."

Even President Bill Clinton was not able to change Assad's mind. The two met in Geneva in March 2000, but Assad continued to insist that without the return of Golan, there would be no peace treaty with Israel.

The Golan Heights is a 40-mile-long, 12-mile wide, boat-shaped strategic high ground that had been the central issue blocking a peace settlement between Israel and Syria since 1967.

That was when Israel took the Golan Heights from Syria in the Six-Day War. Israel was determined to hang on to the territory; Syria was just as determined to win it back. Hafez Assad refused to do more than devote rhetoric to negotiating a treaty with Israel as long as Israel held on to the Heights.

Standing on the Golan Heights, a visitor can see the flat expanse of land that separates the promontory from Damascus, 40 miles away. Israel fears that if the ground is returned to Syria, the Syrians might use it to shell Israeli settlements, as they had in the past. Syria was just as fearful that the Israelis would use the Golan as a jumping off point to invade Syria.

The Israelis made the Golan fruitful during their occupation. They grew fruits and vegetables among the rugged hills, including grapes for a highly praised wine. Where Syrian guns once pointed at Israel, cattle and sheep grazed. About

Golan Heights, 2000

An Israeli soldier surveys the snow-covered Golan Heights from his post on Mt. Hermon. Syria has set the return of the strategic plateau captured by Israel in the 1967 war as the price of peace and normal relations between the two nations.

15,000 people established 32 settlements on the fertile land.

On the southern end, the farmers cultivated plums, apricots, nectarines, mangoes, grapefruit, bananas, dates, and avocados. On the northern end orchards of apples, pears, peaches, and cherries, and blueberry fields thrived. The farmers also grew cotton, corn, tomatoes, and onions. Dairy cattle dined on the lush grasses.

Manufacturing plants, producing many products—from machinery to film to food packaging to tiles, wall coverings, shoes, and many other goods—were also built on the Heights.

Before the terrorist bombings and killings in the continuing struggle between the Israelis and Palestinians, the Israelis promoted the Heights as a tourist attraction. Visitors enjoyed spectacular scenery, waterfalls, and snow. The Golan Heights was the only area under Israeli control where snow could be found. Mt. Hermon on the northern end is 9,232 feet high and offered a year-round chairlift for skiers.

The Heights is also the site of the Crusader fortress of Ka'alat Namrud and a number of archaeological sites.

Another reason why the Israelis wanted to hang on to the heights was water. When Syria had occupied the territory, it had tried to dry out the Jewish state by diverting the sources of the Jordan River. Israelis say that whoever occupies the region controls a third of Israel's water supply.

In a dry and thirsty land, that's important, even crucial.

Under the administration of Israeli prime minister Ehud Barak, the Israeli government talked about the possibility of vacating the Golan Heights, except for a narrow strip along the Sea of Galilee.

When President Clinton presented this offer to Hafez Assad, the Syrian leader rejected it out of hand. "That is the place I know as the border between Israel and Syria," he told the president. "Up until 1967, I would swim in the Sea of Galilee. I would have barbecues. I ate fish."

Two new presidents, George W. Bush of the United States and Hafez's son Bashar, were the inheritors of the seemingly impossible standoff over the Golan Heights. They would have their turn at trying to make a breakthrough.

Meanwhile, a strong indication that Bashar Assad wants better relations with the United States came in an interview with the Knight Ridder News Service in June 2002. In that interview he discussed how, just a few months earlier, Syria has provided intelligence to the United States about Osama bin Laden's al-Qaeda terrorist network, which was responsible for the attacks on the United States that occurred on September 11, 2001.

Assad said information his country provided to the United States three months earlier had saved the lives of American soldiers who would have been the victims of yet another terrorist attack. Although he declined to give specifics, he said that if the terrorist operation had been successful, it would have killed many American soldiers.

In articles published by Knight Ridder-owned newspapers on June 19, 2002, Assad complained that despite this cooperation, Syria continued to be identified by the United States as a country that sponsors terrorism. He said his aim is to get his country off that list.

A U.S. intelligence official confirmed that Syria had cooperated in U.S. anti-terrorist efforts, but declined to provide details. "The Syrians have been cooperative and supportive in the fight against al-Qaeda, including providing useful information and providing threat information," the official was quoted as saying.

Another intelligence official confirmed that Mohammed Haydar Zammar, a German citizen born in Syria, who helped recruit Mohamed Atta and other September 11 airplane hijackers in Hamburg, is in Syrian custody. There were indications that Syrian authorities may have allowed U.S. intelligence agents to question Zammar about his activities.

These recent events seem to indicate Syria's willingness to help the United States crack down on terrorists, which could lead to Syria's removal from the list of countries sponsoring terrorism and mark the beginning for that country to play a role in the struggle for peace in the Middle East.

Gallery of Photographs
from Syria

Gallery 1
Damascus

Damascus, the capital of Syria, is perhaps the oldest continuously inhabited city in the world. Its beginnings go back to a time before recorded history.

Damascus has been conqueror and conquered, wealthy and destitute. In the 21st century, it is a major metropolis of the Middle East.

These photographs of Damascus, taken between the 1890s and the 1920s, are important because there are so few photographic images of the city during this period. Most of the photographs were taken by tourists and eventually deposited with Britain's Royal Geographical Society.

Muslim Cemetery, 1891

Abusseliman, Pasha of Damascus (right), at Ceremonies Before the Hajj, 1906

A factor in the continuing prosperity of Damascus was the annual pilgrimage (Hajj) to Mecca and Medina. Each year a great caravan, under the command of the Pasha (Ottoman governor) of Damascus, left for the Muslim holy cities. Pilgrims spent weeks in Damascus preparing themselves before the caravan set out.

Street Scene, Damascus, c. 1906

Mosque, Damascus, c. 1915

Country Women in the Courtyard of the Umayyad Mosque, c. 1929

Street Scene, Damascus, c. 1935

Gertrude Bell (1868–1926)

Gertrude Bell, an English traveler and explorer and a prolific writer, was instrumental in determining the borders of the new nation of Iraq and in choosing its first ruler, Prince Feisal I (1921). For years, she was his closest personal and political adviser, a position that earned her the title of "Uncrowned Queen of Iraq."

Bell made many exploratory trips through the Middle Eastern deserts. In 1905, without the permission of local Turkish authorities, she began an unprecedented trip to ancient ruins within present-day Syria. These photographs, which Bell donated to the Royal Geographical Society, were the first taken of these ancient ruins.

Baghdad Gate, Ar-Raqqah, 1905

Ar-Raqqah is an ancient town in northern Syria on the bank of the Euphrates River. Mongol invasions in the 13th century destroyed most of the city.

Architectural Detail, Hauran Area, Southern Syria, 1905

This area of volcanic desolation is interspersed with land well suited to agriculture. This region of southern Syria has more ancient remains than almost anywhere in the Middle East—some three hundred towns and villages have been counted. Virtually all structures built in the Hauran used basalt, one of the hardest materials known.

Ancient Mosque Near Jabal Sais, 1905

At the foot of Jabal Sais mountain are a number of Umayyad remains from the early eighth century, including a castle and this mosque. This area, in the center of a desert, is some one hundred miles east of Damascus.

Ancient Hammam, Jabal Sais, 1905

A Hammam is a bathhouse. Used for sociallizing and relaxation as well as bathing, hammams still exist throughout the Islamic world.

Aleppo

Aleppo is the principal city of northern Syria and the second largest city in the country (after Damascus). It is among the oldest continuously inhabited cities in the world. Aleppo is located about 60 miles distant from both the Mediterranean Sea (west) and the Euphrates River (east). The city was once part of the Ottoman Empire (1516–1918.)

These photographs were taken in the early 1920s. During these years, Aleppo faced a serious economic crisis. The new frontiers imposed by the creation of modern Syria severed links with cities Aleppo had traded with for centuries.

Citadel, Aleppo, c. 1920

The old section of Aleppo is built around this 12th-century citadel. The monumental entrance road crosses a moat which could be flooded at will.

Arab Weavers, Aleppo, c. 1920

Men Smoking Hookahs, Aleppo, c. 1920

A hookah is a tobacco pipe with a long flexible tube by which the smoke is drawn through a jar of water and thus cooled.

Muslim Boys with Saluki Dog, Aleppo, c. 1920

Friday Bazaar (marketplace) at the Citadel, Aleppo, c. 1920

Armenians in Aleppo, c. 1915

The history of the Armenian people is said to date back to the sixth century B.C. and can be traced to a specific geographic area in northeastern Anatolia, centered around Mount Ararat. Armenia was the first nation to make Christianity its official religion. This was done in the early part of the third century A.D. The Armenian people have developed their own national, cultural, and linguistic identity, which has enabled them to survive numerous periods of occupation and persecution.

The horrible Armenian genocide of 1915, with its more than one million victims, led to the exodus of the Armenians from Turkey. Many survivors found refuge in Syria, especially in Aleppo. Today, about 75 percent of the approximately 250,000 Armenians who live in Syria reside in Aleppo.

Armenians are the largest unassimilated ethnic group in Syria. They retain many of their own customs, maintain their own schools, and read newspapers in their own language. Most Armenian leaders have adamantly opposed assimilation and stress the need to maintain an Armenian identity.

These five photographs were taken by G. Patterson, a intrepid British traveler. They were taken within months of the Armenian exodus to Aleppo, circa 1915.

Armenians in Aleppo, c. 1915

Armenian Children in Aleppo, c. 1915

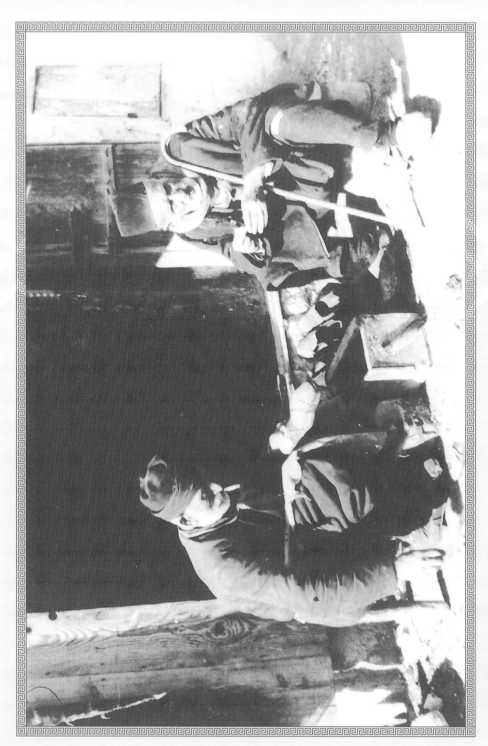

Armenian Men in Aleppo, c. 1915

Armenian Man Spinning Fiber in Aleppo, c. 1915

1516	Ottoman Turks add Syria to their empire.
1914	Syrians and other Arabs revolt against Turks.
1916	Sykes-Picot Agreement; Britain and France divide up Middle East.
1917	Balfour Declaration, granting Jews a homeland in Palestine.
1918	T.E. Lawrence and British troops march into Damascus.
1920	France receives Syria as a League of Nations mandate.
1936	First Syrian national government established under French.
1940	Germany conquers France, sets up Vichy government.
1944	United States and Soviet Union recognize Syria and Lebanon as sovereign states.
1945	French bombard Damascus to quash uprising.
1946	Syria becomes independent country when French pull out.
1947	British stop refugee ship *Exodus*, send Jewish refugees to Germany.
1947	United Nations partitions Palestine into Jewish and Arab states.
1947	Jews proclaim State of Israel; five Arab countries attack.
1947	United States first to recognize Israel; Soviet Union follows.
1948	Arabs attack Israel; Israel victorious; armistice agreements signed.
1949	Military overthrows Syrian government; first of many coups.
1958	Syria joins Egypt in United Arab Republic.
1961	Syria withdraws from United Arab Republic.
1967	Israel defeats Syria, Egypt, and Jordan in Six-Day War.
1967	Israel takes Golan Heights from Syria.
1970	Hafez Assad becomes president of Syria.
1973	Syria and Egypt attack Israel on Yom Kippur.
1976	Syrian troops enter Lebanon to put down civil war.
1979	Israel and Egypt sign peace treaty.
1979	United States adds Syria to list of countries that support terrorists.
1982	Suppression of Muslim Brotherhood.

1982 Israel invades Lebanon to attack PLO bases; clashes with Syrians.

1982 Ronald Reagan sends marines into Lebanon to keep order.

1983 Terrorist bomb kills 241 marines in Beirut.

1984 Marines pull out of Lebanon.

1990 Syria joins U.S.-sponsored coalition to oust Iraq from Kuwait.

2000 Hafez Assad dies; son, Bashar, becomes president of Syria.

Beaton, Margaret. *Syria*. Children's Press, 1988. (For young readers.)

Haag, Michael. *Syria and Lebanon*. Globe Pequot Press, 2000.

Hopwood, Derek. *Syria, 1945–1986: Politics and Society*. Unwin, 1988.

Humphreys, Andrew, and Damien Simonis. *Lonely Planet: Syria: A Travel Survivor Kit*. Lonely Planet Publications, 1999.

Seale, Patrick. *Assad of Syria: The Struggle for the Middle East*. University of California Press, 1990.

Ziser, Eyal. *Assad's Legacy: Syria in Transition*. New York University Press, 2000.

Dayan, Moshe. *Story of My Life.* New York: William Morrow & Co., 1976.

Congressional Quarterly. *The Middle East.* Washington, D.C.: Congressional Quarterly, 1991.

Elon, Amos. *The Israelis: Fathers and Sons.* New York: Holt, Rinehart & Winston, 1971.

Eytan, Walter. *The First Ten Years, A Political History of Israel.* New York: Simon & Schuster, 1958.

Gilbert, Martin. *Churchill.* New York: Henry Holt & Co., 1991.

Graves, Robert. *Lawrence and the Arabian Adventure.* New York: Doubleday, Doran & Co., 1928.

Lawrence, T.E. *Seven Pillars of Wisdom.* New York: Doubleday, Doran & Co., 1935.

O'Brien, Conor Cruise. *The Siege.* New York: Simon & Schuster, 1986.

Shimoni, Yaacov, and Evyatar Levine. *Political Dictionary of the Middle East in the 20th Century.* New York: Quadrangle/The New York Times Book Co., 1974.

Shlaim, Avi. *War and Peace in the Middle East.* New York: Penguin Books, 1995.

Stewart, Desmond. *The Middle East: Temple of Janus.* New York: Doubleday & Co., 1971.

Thubron, Colin. *Mirror to Damascus.* New York: Little Brown & Co., 1967.

Cover: Royal Geographical Society
Frontispiece: Royal Geographical Society

page:

16:	Map courtesy of the Central Intelligence Agency. Available through the website at University of Texas at Austin.	18:	AP/Wide World Photos
		22:	AP/Wide World Photos
		26:	AP/Wide World Photos
		65:	AP/Wide World Photos
17:	Map courtesy of the Central Intelligence Agency. Available through the website at University of Texas at Austin.	97:	AP/Wide World Photos
		103:	AP/Wide World Photos
		108:	AP/Wide World Photos
		113:	AP/Wide World Photos

Unless otherwise credited all photographs in this book © Royal Geographical Society.
No reproduction of images without permission.
Royal Geographical Society
1 Kensington Gore
London SW7 2AR

Unless otherwise credited the photographs in this book are from the Royal Geographical Society Picture Library. Most are being published for the first time.

The Royal Geographical Society Picture Library provides an unrivaled source of over half a million images of the peoples and landscapes from around the globe. Photographs date from the 1840s onwards on a variety of subjects including the British Colonial Empire, deserts, exploration, indigenous peoples, landscapes, remote destinations, and travel.

Photography, beginning with the daguerreotype in 1839, is only marginally younger than the Society, which encouraged its explorers to use the new medium from its earliest days. From the remarkable mid-19th century black-and-white photographs to color transparencies of the late 20th century, the focus of the collection is not the generic stock shot but the portrayal of man's resilience, adaptability and mobility in remote parts of the world.

In organizing this project, we have incurred many debts of gratitude. Our first, though, is to the professional staff of the Picture Library for their generous assistance, especially to Joanna Wright, Picture Library Manager.

JOHN MORRISON is a longtime Philadelphia newspaperman. He has worked as a reporter, rewriteman, and editor. He has published poetry and short stories and has edited several novels for a Dell Publishing Company subsidiary.

AKBAR S. AHMED holds the Ibn Khaldun Chair of Islamic Studies at the School of International Service of American University. He is actively involved in the study of global Islam and its impact on contemporary society. He is the author of many books on contemporary Islam, including *Discovering Islam: Making Sense of Muslim History and Society,* which was the basis for a six-part television program produced by the BBC called *Living Islam.* Ahmed has been a visiting professor and the Stewart Fellow in the Humanities at Princeton University, as well as a visiting professor at Harvard University and Cambridge University.